Requiem for a Village

A History of
the Village of Monkstown

Roddie Andrews

Roddie Andrews has asserted his moral right under the Copyright, Designs and Patents Act 1988 to be identified as the author of this book.
© Copyright 1998 by Roddie Andrews

Published by: Hollybank Publications
28 Kings Avenue, Newtownabbey, Co Antrim, BT37 ODD
Designed and Originated by Jim Barker
Printed by Graphic 3, Belfast

All rights reserved. No part of this work may be produced in any material form (including photocopying or sorting it in any medium by electronic means) without the written permission of the copyright owner except in accordance with the provisions of the Copyright, Designs and Patents Act 1988. Any unauthorised act in this respect may lead to legal proceedings, including a Civil claim for damages.

ISBN 0 9535088 0 3

Contents

CHAPTER 1	A Short History	7
CHAPTER 2	At Work	21
CHAPTER 3	At Play	34
CHAPTER 4	The Travelling Picture-Man	49
CHAPTER 5	The Salvation of Taghera	56
CHAPTER 6	Shops and Services	62
CHAPTER 7	The Last Refuge of a Scoundrel	75
CHAPTER 8	The Changing Village	83
CHAPTER 9	Black Sandy's Hat Trick	98
CHAPTER 10	Rocking into the Sixties	107
CHAPTER 11	Confessions of a Counter-Jumper	123
CHAPTER 12	The End of the Show	133
CHAPTER 13	Monkstown Revisited — and some Reflections	147
Coloured pics APPENDIX	A Walk through Monkstown Village of the 1940s and 50s	167
Acknowledgement		171

*To
Mary and Jim*

6 Requiem for a Village

CHAPTER 1
A Short History

The village of Monkstown lay on a plain between two hills — Knockagh to the north and Carnmoney Hill to the south-west. It was in an attractive setting, completely surrounded by fields and nearby was a small wood known locally as 'The Plantin'.

Originally a townland in the parish of Carnmoney, Monkstown's southern and western boundary is the Three Mile River, which in those days linked various mill dams before eventually flowing into the sea at Whiteabbey. The northern and eastern boundary could follow approximately the Belfast-Derry railway line which had a halt at Monkstown.

Throughout the nineteenth century various mills sprang up along the Three Mile River. In the earlier period the water was dammed and used to drive large wooden waterwheels, which in turn powered the mill machinery. In the later 1860s-1870s the river would provide a ready source of water for steam-driven power. The Ordnance Survey Memoirs of Ireland County Antrim *1, Vol 2, Institute of Irish Studies, QUB, 1990* (editors: Day, A. and McWilliams, P.) notes that in 1828 a calico print works was situated in the townland of Monkstown and that it afforded employment for 200 hands of whom 190 were male and 10 were female. The various processes involved in the linen industry, spinning, weaving and bleaching would all take place in mills, factories and bleaching greens along the Three Mile River valley.

The mills and factories could not rely solely on the inhabitants of the surrounding countryside for their workforces. Hence the country village grew up around the means of production. This was typical of the time across Ulster. Many of these villages would be built by the mill owners who might also help to finance the building of a local schoolhouse. A drawback of this system was that when you lost your job you had to leave the factory house — a double discipline.

Early Nineteenth Century

Monkstown's history is bound up with the development of the Parish of Carnmoney. The Ordnance Survey Memoirs of Ireland (Ibid.) are regarded as a Domesday Book and their records provide us with a picture of what life was like in the 1830s.

Apparently most of our ancestors were Scots, having arrived in Carnmoney around the early seventeenth century — mainly soldiers and their families probably connected with the garrison at Carrickfergus (about six miles to the east of the parish). Almost two hundred years later the accent was still being noticed as *quaint and broad* with Scottish sayings and phrases prevailing especially among old folk.

The census of 1831 has 995 families, consisting of 5423 individuals, living in the parish. Of these families 394 were employed in agriculture and 316 in trade, manufacture or handicrafts. So, generally speaking, the inhabitants of Monkstown at this time, gentry aside, probably came from backgrounds of agriculture or manufacture.

The development of the parish owes a lot to Nicholas Grimshaw and his sons. James Hargreaves and Richard Arkwright had patented their spinning inventions in 1764 and 1769 respectively. Robert Joy, uncle of Henry Joy McCracken, had toured mills in the North of England in 1777 and as a result of this trip installed, in the Belfast Poorhouse, the necessary machinery to teach the children in the house to spin and weave cotton (see *The Life and Times of Mary Ann McCracken*. Allen Figgis (1960); McNeill, Mary.) The young Nicholas Grimshaw, just arrived in Ireland from Lancashire in 1778, was interested in Joy's experiment and he built the first mill in this country for spinning cotton thread at Whitehouse. He was a man concerned for the welfare of his workers and built houses for them leading to the creation of a village there. This work was extended later by his sons and a schoolhouse was added. They established a lending library in the school too in 1834 and supplied over 146 texts and provided other books used for instruction.

The introduction of cotton spinning and cotton printing brought about large improvements in the parish in terms of work, not solely for the local unemployed, but also attracting people from all parts of County Antrim and as far afield as Derry and Tyrone. Thus a stimulus was given to agriculture due to more money now in circulation. At this time Carnmoney was the main source of supply to Belfast of butter and buttermilk. Now increased demands for meal and potatoes meant more farmers starting to till what had hitherto been wasteland. Other manufactories soon followed the Grimshaw example and set up in the area. Many of the mills that arrived were built on the former sites of corn mills. This was the case with the calico print works owned by John and William Henry Cooper at Monkstown (mentioned previously). Previous to 1828 it was a corn mill owned by John Thompson of Jennymount. Nicholas Grimshaw, the founder of cotton spinning in Ireland, died in 1805 and is buried at Carnmoney.

It should be remembered that Belfast was only starting to develop as an industrial town at this time, having been more concerned with commerce and shipping. (The population in 1782 is given as 13,105.) The mail coach maintained a link between Carnmoney Parish and Belfast, passing through Whitehouse at 8am to take the main turnpike road to Carrickfergus and Larne, then returning again through the village at 5pm.

The Survey (Ibid.) notes that the agricultural workers were: *rather prone to whiskey drinking* and that they: *never omit an opportunity of indulging in it. There was too great a facility for it.* Apparently there were eighteen spirit shops in the parish. Of the mill workers it says: *they are too prone to whiskey drinking and much of the women's earnings are squandered in tea.* (!)

The cotton print workers came in for a special vitriol. The cause was 'combination' or 'trade (union) disputes'. We are told that several strikes had taken place among the printers and their obstinacy in refusing to come to terms was encouraged by the assistance which they received from the 'trade' (known today as secondary picketing). The system of combination became so formidable that the Grimshaws gave up their cotton printing business in 1834 and converted their premises to flax spinning mills. This was the case at Mossley.

Apparently the character of the mill workers improved with the departure of the cotton printers and the Survey (Ibid.) states that: *the system of combination not merely afforded a bad example but kept up a continual excitement among the work people.* It also adds very significantly that: *being tenants of their employers is the cause of a salutary check being kept over them,* i.e. out of a job meant out of the company house.

The housing in Monkstown of this period (1836-39) is reported as follows:

Attached to the factories in the townland of Monkstown are several rows of neat cottages, built for their work people by the proprietors of these establishments. The Survey (Ibid.) notes that they are neat and superior to the accommodation provided for agricultural labourers. They are slate-roofed, two apartment buildings. An example of these types of dwellings would probably have been Spout Row. The larger houses in the village would not be built until some time later when the steam powered factory was built.

Amusement it seems consisted mainly of dancing. *Reels, country dances and quadrilles* were usually accompanied by fiddlers (and probably whiskey). *The refreshments consist of punch and biscuits.* We are told: *they dance pretty well and lightly,* but that: *the dances got up among the factory people are not by any means conducted with the same propriety as those at the farmers' houses.*

Spout Row in the 1960s. — Courtesy of Newtownabbey Times.

Monkstown in the 1940s onwards

The village of Monkstown as I knew it probably dated from around the time of the building of the local factory as a steam driven enterprise — very likely around 1860 onwards. The factory was derelict when we came to live beside it in March 1944, but the factory owners — the Henderson Family — also owned the house we lived in, one of a tall terrace of houses in the mill yard. Unlike some villages which had their houses closely grouped around the mill, Monkstown's dwellings were not so homogeneous. In the Appendix we take a walk through the village of the 1940s and the reader can find this on page 167. A map of the area is located on the inside of the back cover.

The old factory buildings were still almost intact when we came to Monkstown but shortly afterwards they suffered major damage during a violent thunderstorm. I

The tall houses in the Mill Yard (1950s). — Courtesy of Belfast Telegraph.

remember as a small child crying out in terror because I thought the house had fallen in and such was my fear that I had to be consoled. This became known as the night the factory 'fell in'. Next day every family in our terrace turned out to salvage timber from the ruins. It was reminiscent of a scene from the Cornish coast, people with armfuls of wooden sheets, like wreckers after descending on a stricken vessel to capture the spoils. But skill was never in short supply. The timber would undergo a remarkable transmutation to reappear as garden sheds or pigeon lofts. The factory machinery had long been removed before the fateful night but I recall a large mill clock lying in a building near the entrance. The main buildings consisted of a large 3-storey black stone building with a flat roof, a 3- or 4-storey stone building with roof and floors collapsed and a new looking red brick structure with roof collapsed, which had been the boiler room. Other smaller buildings adjoined these main structures. A curious feature of this factory was that the chimney did not emanate through the roof of the main buildings.

Instead, the tall stack stood some distance away in a nearby field. (The site of the present Adare Park.) It was connected to the factory by an underground tunnel.

I knew four people who had worked in the old factory. One was a neighbour living in the mill terrace, Mrs Charlotte Peake, known to us as Granny Peake. She was an institution herself in those days, a great old character. Another lady who worked in the factory was Mrs William Ramsay who lived across the river from us. The third was Joe Boyd, a good friend of mine, who lived in School Row. Joe had done a spell in the factory. Evidently there were a lot of women employed there and weaving processes did require mainly female labour. Finally there was Miss Rosetta Ferguson who lived in Black Row. She was the aunt of the Sharpe family and was a kind, gentle woman. The factory ceased working about 1928.

The demise of the remaining factory buildings took place in the early 1960s. A group of dilutees, who knew as much about demolition work as the rest of us know about crocodile breeding, undertook the job. They even tackled the mill chimney — one of the tallest of its kind in Ireland! Such was the state of their unpreparedness that a neighbour of ours had to shout a warning to them when he saw the stack shudder and they had to jump clear at risk to their lives. Their coats are still buried to this day beneath the rubble. I wonder what Fred Dibnah (the celebrated steeplejack) would have made of that. However, such was the undignified end of Monkstown's old mill which had once been the hub of the community.

Education in Monkstown has a history of going back over many years to the early nineteenth century. The following is an excerpt taken from Ordnance Survey Memoirs of Ireland, County Antrim 1 Vol. 2, *Institute of Irish Studies, QUB, 1990* (editors: Day, A. and McWilliams, P.) under the heading Private Schools. 'Held in an excellent suitable house measuring 16 feet by 15 feet, built for the purpose by subscription, situated in the townland of Monkstown; established in 1800, house rebuilt in 1820; income from pupils £15; expenditure on salaries £15; Intellectual instruction: spelling, reading, writing, *Thompson and Gough's Arithmetics, Jackson's Book-keeping, Knowle's Elocutionist, Manson's Primer and Spelling Book ...'* Moral instruction was by two Presbyterian Ministers. A total of 34 pupils attended: 33 Presbyterians, one Roman Catholic and the Master Robert Gourley, Presbyterian.

Mrs Charlotte Bradley, a former Librarian at Monkstown Public Library has put together a history of the old school. The school mentioned above was probably the forerunner of the National School that was built in 1854. The public elementary school — the name changed after the birth of the Northern Ireland state — had Mr Tom Kirkpatrick as headmaster for many years until his retirement in 1944. He was a good teacher I am told but very strict. The building had three classrooms until 1937 when a fourth was added. This was the situation when I attended in 1945. Another link with the old factory was

16 Requiem for a Village

Monkstown National School (built 1854). The school stands beside Riverside Terrace. The building was replaced on the same site by a public elementary school years later. — Courtesy of Abbey Historical Society.

formed. During one of its periods of renovation or extension the school moved to temporary premises in a large room in the old mill. I have spoken to several people who attended the place during this period and I believe it occurred sometime around 1937. By the time I had started school (1945) Jimmy Stewart had replaced Tom Kirkpatrick as headmaster. In 1957 (after my time) another two classrooms, an assembly hall and a servery were built providing accommodation for 240 pupils. The school was now a primary school. In 1970 pupils transferred to Hollybank Primary School in the Monkstown Estate and now the old school is used as a music centre for the southern area of the NEELB. Still there are links with the past.

Mrs Singer, a very popular teacher during my school days in the old building, became vice-principal of Hollybank Primary.

Community life in the old village was also centred near the factory. In the mill terrace where we lived there were six houses, but the sixth house was larger than the others with different sized windows. This part of our building had originally been used, mainly as offices for the factory, and also as a recreation hall. Dances were held in there from time to time. It cannot have held a very large crowd — probably a small local hop with a couple of fiddles playing. I remember one old-timer telling me about leaving a girl home from one of these dances. He said he remembered kissing her beneath a gas lamp which had stood somewhere near the corner of our front garden. It was many years later when my father and I were digging the foundations for a garage that my spade struck something metal. We unearthed it and sure enough it was the metal base of the ancient gas lamp standard, exactly where the old man had said it was.

The name Monkstown has very ancient origins. It is said to have taken its title from an old church which was situated just off Knockagh Road near an ancient graveyard. Nothing is known locally of the origin, history or date or cause of its destruction but excavations, which took place about 1836 to a depth of six feet, revealed pieces of cut stone and timber which bore the marks of fire.

Some called this church an abbey and it is believed a village inhabited by monks stood close by it, and it is this circumstance which gave the church and townland its name.

Monkstown village as it looked in the 1940s and 50s. Elsie Hagan's Post Office and James Hagan's shop can both be seen on the right.

There are regal connections with the area according to tradition. It is thought that King Fergus, who is said to be the first king of Scotland and also a king of Ireland, and who reigned about 320 years before the birth of Christ, is buried in the old church of Monkstown. Since he lived and reigned over 300 years before Christianity he cannot therefore have been buried in a church. Campion in his *History of Ireland* refers to a tradition that Fergus, in coming from Scotland to drink the mineral waters of a well in Carrickfergus, was drowned and his body washed ashore three miles west of the town. He was buried at Monkstown alias Monksland where there is a burial place and the ruins of a small chapel. So the tradition cannot be true as no chapel could have existed there at that time, but perhaps he was buried where the abbey later stood.

All that remains of that ancient church is the ivy-covered western gable and the foundations, almost grown over. They stand in the old Monkstown cemetery. The last two people from the village to be buried in the graveyard were Sammy Currie, in March 1956 and his wife Jane the following November. I remember the couple well and was in their house a few times. They lived in the end house of White Row and Sammy was a familiar sight standing at his door smoking a pipe.

I last visited the old cemetery in 1981 and at that time nature was fast reclaiming it with much of the graveyard overgrown. On a previous visit in the 1950s I recall seeing many pauper graves of complete families wiped out by the potato famine. Only a small piece of slate marked their last resting place. Poverty even in death!

The Turnstile (1996). Used by Bleachgreen workers walking from Monkstown to Whiteabbey. — Photograph: William Andrews.

CHAPTER 2
At Work

Awake in the early morning I lay listening to the echoes of footsteps on the loose stony avenue down past our house. I could pick out the distinctive sound of Alec Brown as he wore wooden-soled clogs. He passed at about 7.30am with others on their way to work in Whiteabbey Bleaching Company at Bleachgreen. They would take a short cut down a narrow path between two hedges called 'The By Wash', cross the Three Mile River by stepping stones (later by a wooden bridge), through a turnstile and out on to the Green Lane to complete their final mile and a half to work. Alec always wore clogs because the area he worked in was usually wet under foot.

To find employment people had to look beyond Monkstown village, to the surrounding villages and to Belfast. Whiteabbey boasted a mill and a factory. Mossley had a large spinning mill owned by Henry Campbell and Company and there was Greeves mill at Whitehouse. None of these places were renowned for paying high wages, they paid 'the going rate', but for many boys and girls leaving school at fourteen this was ambition enough. If you had an older brother, sister or parent in the mill they could approach the foreman or

School Row (left) and facing it is the old public elementary school (with the tall chimney). Riverside Terrace is on the right beyond the school. — Courtesy of Abbey Historical Society.

forewoman and after a brief interview you got a start — no GCSEs required.

    Many women, girls and some young men opted for Mossley mill. The firm had a bus service which collected workers in the village in the morning about 7.45am and returned them again at 5.50pm. In those days everyone travelled by bus. Some women and girls were fortunate enough to gain employment in Gallaher's tobacco factory in York Street, Belfast where the financial rewards were higher. A few men worked there also. A familiar sight in those days would be a man carrying an Oxo tin to work containing his 'piece' (i.e. sandwiches). These flimsy light aluminium boxes would be supplied free by the local grocer. Most men travelled to Belfast to work, many employed in the shipyard. Others would work in Mackie's engineering works or Short and Harland's aircraft factory or maybe Sirocco Works. The shipyard workers would catch a bus leaving the village around 7am alighting in Belfast to catch the tram (or later a red bus) to take them down to Queen's Island in time to start work at 8am.

    Like a muezzin calling the faithful to prayer the mill horns would sound across the fields announcing the commencement of work but also reminding us kids that it was time to rise and shine. In a large family you learn independence early in life. I was the middle child of seven. When we had got ourselves ready, supervised by my mother, our sandwich lunches would be packed into our school bags and off we would set. We were always on the road early but we would call for our chums on the way. By the time we arrived at the crossroads and met other school mates quite a crowd would be in our group. Boys tended to be with boys, girls with girls, but within our groups there would be a wide cross-section of ages from final year students to first year. This is something not possible today because of the change to second level education at eleven plus.

The public elementary school day commenced at 9am (or was it 9.15am?). A pupil would be detailed to ring the school bell at this time. These were the days of the standard system. The elementary curriculum was spread over seven standards starting at the lowest, first standard. As you entered the school at the boys' entrance the first classroom was presided over by Mrs McCoubrey who taught first and second standards. Next classroom (where I abode) was Mrs McCullough's junior and senior infants. You started in the junior class at four years of age. A Mrs Gallagher shortly replaced the much-loved Mrs McCullough who retired. The third classroom was Mrs Singer's who taught third and fourth standards and the last classroom was the schoolmaster's James Stewart, who taught fifth, sixth and seventh standards. The subjects taught at different levels across the standards were: reading, writing, arithmetic (including geometry), spelling, grammar, geography, history, hygiene, singing and drawing. Geography was limited to that of the British Empire — the pink patches on the atlas. History was restricted to the reign of the Tudors, local history not even being alluded to at all. On a Thursday afternoon boys of twelve years and over went to Whiteabbey Technical School for woodwork while the girls remained for cookery.

With the boiler stove stoked up lessons would begin. I cannot recall a lot about these early days in the infant classes. One thing that stands out is being taught to read using a very tattered, well-worn, thin children's reading text. It was well illustrated. A story concerned a conversation between the wind, the rain and the sun about how they could induce a man walking down a road to remove his coat. The wind blew fiercely and violently but the man pulled his coat tighter around him. Then the rain lashed heavily with as little success. Finally the sun shone, warm and radiant, and the man divested his coat. I suppose the moral was supposed to be that violent action does not work whereas gentle persuasion will. Another feature was a little poem 'There was a crooked man who walked a crooked mile' etc, with a picture of a crooked little man with a wobbly looking walking stick. The alphabet we learned by rote.

Mid-morning brings a break. A buzz of children's voices is heard as the small bottles of milk are distributed along with the straws. The lady teachers retire for a cup of tea; at least one of the teachers smoked because I recall on one occasion seeing a red packet with a black cat emblem being deposited in a handbag after the break.

Lessons recommence with the topic of number. A large abacus stands on one side of the classroom. It is rarely, if ever, used. One class gathers around the blackboard and the 'times tables' are recited. I can still recall the sing-song way the children's voices rhyme off these tables. 'Two twos are four, two threes are six' etc.

Eventually the time wears around to the lunch break. There is no canteen in the school, only a room — Mrs Singer's — where packed lunches can be taken. There is no tea or soft drinks. Children living locally go home for lunch. I remember some years later a prank being played in the lunch room by a senior boy. He put carbide into an ink well in one of the school-desks. Immediately a spout of ink shot up and hit the ceiling leaving a blue stain on the white emulsion. The master threatened a flogging but nobody squealed.

It is a sunny day so I have my lunch outside in the school playground. As soon as the food is taken games commence. Amid laughter and shouts we divide (i.e. the boys) into two teams for the rough horseplay game of cops and robbers. These are times when new friendships are forged (and new enemies made). During the latter part of the lunch break the headmaster Mr Stewart patrols the playground with the cane hooked into a trouser pocket at his side like a sword ready to administer instant justice. All ball games are prohibited, I assume in the interest of preserving window panes. This is an unwritten law. Woe betide anyone caught at this moment kicking football. In our school play area are two Anderson air raid shelters left over from war time. It is strictly taboo to climb on to the roofs of these buildings. It was some few years later that I and a few others broke this law. The headmaster came on the scene and ordered the offenders down for punishment. I did not think I had been spotted so I lay flat down on the roof until the coast was clear then joined the throng heading into school. The offenders were lined up for 'two of the best'. At this moment a little sneak pointed me out to the headmaster. My face gave me away. The principal did not like to be outsmarted. I received four strokes for being 'too clever'. However that was in the future, today the school bell rings and I return with others to the infant classroom.

In the afternoons the 'babies' (junior infants) played with Plasticine and the senior infants worked at making raffia mats, a type of plate mat made from weaving coloured fibre on to a perforated sturdy base. Others worked at cutting out coloured geometrical shapes of cardboard and pasting these on to dark paper, of the type found in photograph albums, to form attractive patterns. This occupied us until the end of lessons. The infant classes broke up earlier than the seniors so we returned home without the company of older brothers and sisters.

Life was hard in those times for large families living on a single wage. My father was a semi-skilled labourer in the Belfast Shipyard. Every penny counted. My mother and he had chosen a hard road. To be successful, and they were, they had to work as a team — a division of labour. She saw the crucial thing was the weekly wage. My father was at the centre of her attention. It was important that his meals were on the table ready when he got home. She attended to all his wants. He relied on her judgement in all matters. Everything indoors was her responsibility; the washing, ironing, baking, cleaning, polishing, cooking, dusting and all the thousand little things that contribute to the smooth running of the household. My mother also administered justice with a leather strap. When we were old enough the children were delegated chores, the shopping, washing and drying dishes and peeling the potatoes. I eventually came in for all three. My father, as well as doing any household repairs, such as mending a broken window pane or fixing a broken chair or table, also tended to all outside work. After his evening meal he was in the vegetable garden with his neat rigs. He grew all our soup and salad vegetables. If there was a shed to be built he could make a tidy job of it although he never worked at joinery as a trade. Also, he kept hens and fresh eggs were always available. He was very skilled at repairing bicycles too. As a couple they had the odd tiff but they lived for each other and for the family and the sun never went down upon their wrath.

The lot of women deserves a special mention. In our terrace we did not have electricity installed until the late 1950s. All cooking had to be done on an iron range in the kitchen. The day which stretched our primitive facilities to the limit was wash day, always a Monday. My mother would be up about 5.30am to get the range fire lit and organise the boiling of lots of water. The wash pot would be bubbling on the range. As soon as she got my father off to work, my mother got stuck in to the washing. A small tin bath was the wash tub with a washboard and Sunlight soap for lather. I seem to remember some of the early soap powders, Rinso and Oxydol, with Colmans starch and a bluebag. On early frosty mornings, scrubbing with hands immersed in water, moving from hot to cold, was hard, grinding work. After rinsing, the washing would be put through the mangle, a machine with two large wooden rollers for squeezing the water from the garments and operated by turning an iron handle at the side. There was a lot of washing, especially with seven children. She would have the first lot out hanging on the line by 8 o'clock. We children did not like washing day. We would come down to breakfast to find the kitchen steamy with water everywhere and my mother bustling about with little time to talk to us. The washing would continue to midday and when we returned from school we would find both clothes lines full and swaying in the breeze. The women would worry about the weather on washdays. Conversations would contain phrases such as 'sure there's no dryin' today' or 'Isn't that a great dryin' day?'. On wet days washing would have to be hung on inside lines to dry. The most part of another day would be spent standing over an ironing board smoothing the washed bed linen and clothes, a back-aching job. All the while the normal chores had to be done too such as making the meals, looking after the baby and so on.

My mother baked twice a week. I looked forward to her midweek baking day. She would bake soda bread, wheaten bread and treacle bread. A circle of dough would be rolled out flat on the flour-dusted breadboard. Then the circle would be cross cut through the centre to make four equal sized farls of bread which she baked on a griddle on the range. Usually home from school in time to witness these operations I would beg my mother to make me a small farl of soda bread from the left over dough. Is there anything to match the appetising smell of home baked bread? As the little farl came off the griddle I had it devoured without ceremony. She would bake wheaten bannocks and soda bannocks also. On Fridays she would do her weekend baking. Pastry and cakes were never bought in our family. My mother baked all these herself. Her *piece de resistance* was her shortbread. We children were spoiled almost by the range of choice. There would be extra cakes and sandwiches baked if we were expecting my aunts and uncles for a visit at the weekend. She was an excellent and versatile cook. In later years the range was replaced by a tiled 'Devon' fireplace and a two-burner oil cooker (Valor), with a detachable oven, was installed in our little scullery.

How primitive life then seems when we look back with the relative comforts of the late 1990s. How tough it was for women. The bedroom floors were covered with linoleum and carpet mats. Cleaning the rooms involved the use of a polishing mop and a mechanical device called a carpet sweeper. Even for houses with electricity a fridge was unheard of in those days. Instead we had a box with a wooden frame and metal gauze windows on all sides. It was called a meat-safe and was used to hold meat, milk, butter, bacon and cheese. The principle of its construction allowed the cool air of the scullery to circulate through the gauze at the same time preventing the intrusion of flies. All the lighting in our house was by paraffin oil lamps. We had a variety of these, double burners, single-burners and small bedroom lamps. My mother had to fill these lamps, trim the wicks and clean the tall chimney globes. The main light in the kitchen was a Tilley pressure oil lamp. Washing facilities were also primitive, the tin bath in front of the range fire for the weekly scrub down. On other days it was the morning wash at the brown sink in the scullery at the cold water tap, winter and summer.

My mother was a clever and resourceful person and she had a good technical education. She was a mine of information. When we were doing our homework we would ask her to spell words or to tell us the capital of such and such a country, etc. She must have felt the stifling of intelligence in the drudgery of her work. Life must have seemed set in concrete but if she saw her future in this way she never complained. Her way of life with the conditions already described would be typical for working class women living in the country. I have no doubt that had my mother been a young married woman today she could have gone to university and obtained a degree. But for women of her time it was not possible — theirs was a life of sacrifice of self and dedication to family.

Mary and Jim (mother and father)

My father was a hard working man who could turn his hand to many skills. He was clever too, finishing top of his class at Kilbride School and was thus selected and proposed by the principal as the student to aspire to a post in the offices of Doagh Spinning Mill. However, like many of his sons, my father could not adapt to working inside and left the office after a couple of weeks. He found work on the farmlands of the Dixon family who lived at Drumadarragh House and it was discovered that he had a way with horses and animals. Before moving to Monkstown he had been land-steward with the Whiteabbey Bleaching Company for a number of years. The company had many fields around Whiteabbey, Bleachgreen and Monkstown under crops during these war time (and post war years). It was my father's responsibility to plough, sow and reap these crops with the help of a few labourers. I remember corn waving in the field which is now the site of Adare Park and Cloyne Crescent in Monkstown. My father drove a large Fordson Major tractor at times alternating to a little grey Ferguson but the work-power also consisted of a couple of Clydesdale horses.

He left the company after a difference with the manager, his cousin, and that resulted in us having to leave the land-steward's house. So we arrived in Monkstown in 1944. Work was scarce in these days. My father got a job as a semi-skilled labourer in the Belfast shipyard of Harland & Wolff. It must have been a culture shock for him after the 'freedom' of the open fields. But he knuckled down to it for the sake of the family and he never complained. I remember years later when I was in the Accounts Department of Harland & Wolff calling down to see him where he worked. He was a blacksmith's helper at this time. I was on my lunch break but he was hard at work and could not stop for a word. The blacksmith was on a piece-rate. My father, on a much lesser rate, had to turn the work piece over with the tongs after each fall of the hammer. The sweat rolled down his forehead. It brought home to me the austerity of it all. Here at a stage of life when we was getting on in years he was having to graft even harder than when he had started in the shipyard back in 1944.

 My parents both denied themselves in the harshness of the time as they struggled against poverty, dirt and ignorance to bring us up respectable, decent, tidy and clean. Their sacrifice was typical of many of that bygone age.

CHAPTER 3

At Play

The bane of my mother's life during our school days was tar. The operation of laying a new surface on the county road was something that had a particular fascination for us children. The appearance of a steamroller and the bewitching smell of the tar would bring us running up to the road. Despite warnings and threats from my mother we were drawn to it as irresistibly as iron filings to a magnet. My brother Billy, myself and our chums would assemble on the footpath beside the mobile brazier. This was in fact a steel wheelbarrow containing a fire of coals into which would be placed the tarry heads of shovels and rakes. This kept the tar stones from sticking to the implements. We watched in delight as a wooden-cabbed lorry drew up and out got the driver with a handle which he used to winch up the lorry's tipping mechanism. The load of tarred stones fell onto the road. Immediately a group of men dressed in dark boiler suits, tucked in at the ankles with a safety pin and wearing very tarry boots, descended on the pile of stones with shovels and rakes and proceeded to level them and spread them along the road. Then the moment we were waiting for, the steam roller hove into view and like a lumbering elephant it descended on the new laid surface. A black sooty figure wrestled with the controls. The fly wheel flew around and the safety valve blew off steam. The road was flattened neatly into place.

Our fixation for anything driven by steam caused us to hang around the roller and our hero the driver all day long. When he drove off to the Green Lane to take on water at a nearby stream we followed to watch the process, giving a hand to place the rubber hose in the water. The steamroller pulled a grey wooden caravan to each new job. The driver, who maybe lived many miles away, stayed overnight in the caravan and thus acted as watchman for the roller. On this occasion he camped at the end of our avenue. You might wonder how it was possible that we managed to get 'clarried' (covered) with tar but we did. Somehow tar had got onto the footpath causing tarry stones to cling to our sandals. We had touched the tarry rakes with our hands and I actually got a thick coating of tarry stones on the seat of my pants!

Another feature of road repair in those days and one rarely documented was the tar-boiler. This was a horse-drawn vehicle used for repairing worn patches or holes in the road. At various points on a grass verge beside the county road would lie a forty gallon drum of tar beside or on top of a pile of fine stones. This was for use by the tar-boiler. The vehicle itself was a glorified kitchen range on wheels with a tall chimney flue. It was fired by coals and had a little crane on top for lifting the drum of tar onto the heating plate. The metal bung of the tar barrel would be unscrewed to be replaced by a metal tap. When the heat of the fire had reduced the viscosity of the tar to running liquid a metal container like a garden watering can would be filled at the tap. The tar would then be poured into any observable hole in the road and a shovel of fine stones would be thrown on top. The horse and tar-boiler would proceed leisurely along the road stopping to examine any suspect patch of surface. There was very little traffic. The man who led the horse and did the tarring was a deep study. He was of a stout stocky build with fat red cheeks. On his head he wore a cloth cap which adapted so well to the shape that it looked like he might have been born with it on. A thick working shirt and waistcoat with shirt sleeves rolled up to reveal two broad sturdy arms, brown corduroy trousers with khaki leggings and a stout pair of boots. He wore a bag apron and around his neck he had a large cotton hanky tied in a carter's knot. When he proceeded to cut a plug of tobacco he displayed a nonchalance and dexterity which bespoke years of practice.

    On our way home from school we would follow the tar-boiler. We would examine the repair. The siren of curiosity proved too strong and I would stretch out a foot to test the firmness. The result — a school shoe covered in sticky tar and grey stones. My mother threatened blue murder.

    During these post war year the horse was a common feature in haulage transport. There was a fuel shortage and petrol was rationed so cars were few on the roads. There was not the same affluence as today. The clank of farmers' rustic stiff carts was an everyday sound as they travelled to and from Belfast. The Duff family — long resident in Monkstown — used horses for their deliveries.

John had his milk round and his brother Bob had a horse-drawn four-wheel cart for the fruit and vegetables business. Bob lived beside us at number 3. His son Bobby Junior also had a fruit and vegetable run of his own in a pony and spring cart. I remember a large Clydesdale horse hauling a load of steaming coal-brick around the village. I had much admiration for these great beasts, so strong yet obedient and faithful. Another part of the scene at this time was the 'rag-man'. He came in a pony and spring cart. His name was Billy Marley and he would exchange pieces of delph crockery for old clothes or rags. He was a decent little man but it is beyond me how he earned a living at this. As a final note in this subject I recall what I believe was the last funeral in Monkstown to have a horse-drawn hearse. I was a child coming home from school when I witnessed the shiny black horses with their plumes. The deceased was a Mrs Luney. The family lived in the little railway house on the Station Road. Their son Tommy went to our school and he was a few years older than me. Even as a child I remember wondering what it would be like if I was to lose my mother and I felt a great sadness for him. It was the fashion at this time that whenever anyone lost a close relative a black diamond shaped piece of cloth would be sewn on the sleeve of a coat to indicate a person in mourning.

To us children the fields around us with their rivers and dams, plantin' and old mill were an adventure playground where imagination and nature intertwined. I loved the river in summer but as a child I had caught rheumatic fever with resultant rheumatic pains and a 'murmur' at the heart. So I was forbidden to swim in the water. The dictum was obeyed when in sight of the house. However across the meadow out of sight of parental eyes there was a bend in the river where the water ran clean and deep. It was here that my chums and I did what American kids call 'skinny-diving'. We could not really swim but we made gallant attempts, larking and splashing about. One of our fears was horse-leeches, a small leech with suckers at either end. A shout of 'horse-leech!' would bring us dashing out of the river. It was tantamount to shouting 'alligator!' We believed these creatures would fasten on to your skin and suck your blood. Wet hair was the thing I had to avoid as this would give away my guilty secret. Wet feet too were taboo. This would happen as a result of walking across the dew-covered meadow. But children's devious nature is also full of invention. I would go into the old factory and cover my canvas 'gutty' shoes with white mortar dust so that any dampness went undetected.

There was a small mill dam at the head of our avenue but we were shrewd enough to avoid the water here. It was deep and dangerous to non-swimmers. However it abounded with wild life. As well as the usual 'spricks' (sticklebacks) it had frogs and tadpoles. The frogs would migrate from a swamp across the road at a certain time of the year. The dam also contained newts. These little amphibian efts would resemble a small lizard and there appeared to be two types of them. Dragonflies and damsel flies would be seen along the dam banks in summer. The only boat ever to appear on the water was built by Eric Marks who lived in the house behind the dam. Her name was painted proudly on the prow, *The Monk*.

At Play

David Andrews standing beside the 'Wee' Dam. The roof of the factory manager's house and the mill chimney are in the background.

Like others of our age we played with hoops using a guiding implement made from bull wire called a 'cleek'.

Bicycles were for the better off; instead 'guiders' were built. The basic version of this was a plank with wooden axle supports at either end. The front axle support swivelled to allow steering by the feet. Four pram wheels were attached to the axles and someone pushed you along. If pram wheels were not available a cheaper version using ball bearings for wheels was used. But this could only run on level concrete surfaces.

The nearby wood or plantin' as it was called was the scene of much of our childhood play. The Three Mile River was lined with beech, ash and chestnut trees and this provided the fringe to a long sloping meadow. In spring the first primroses and the yellow lesser celandine would grow around the bank at the foot of the trees bringing early colour to the still bare woods. It was a place where fancy ran free. Our boyish games with older brothers and chums might be a re-enactment of the battles of Robin Hood and the notorious Sheriff of Nottingham. We would climb the chestnut trees and play with self-made bows and arrows. Later a boy in the village lost an eye due to being struck with an arrow. We did not have to be told to desist from this practice. Imagination would transport us to the wild west. The river was the Little Big Horn and the sloping meadow the scene of Custer's Last Stand. We would charge down the hill to be 'mown down' by invisible Red Indians, rolling over 'mortally wounded', with the most realistic groans. Being country children we knew not to tramp down the tall grass once the hay making time came around. However once the grass was cut and the hay ricked it was ours again. Children's feet, boys and girls, would dash among the trees and ricks at hide and

The 'Big' Dam with swans in winter. Black Row, Riverside Terrace and School Row are seen in the background.

seek or tig. On other occasions Granny McNeily, our next door neighbour at number 2, would take me and her two grandsons farther afield on a picnic to Sunshine Meadow near Hollybank. This was the only field in the area to have a name. Naming fields is traditional in Ireland. We picked 'vitchy peas' (common vetch) from the grassy banks and sour leeks from the fields.

A small stream ran tributary to the Three Mile River, having their confluence on the edge of the plantin'. This was known simply as 'The Burn River'. Its source was on the Knockagh Hill and it flowed through the village past Riverside Terrace and Black Row to pass underneath the old factory and emerge at two white pillars near the woods. This was a very clean little stream and we used to try and catch the small trout as they slipped through our hands to dart away under rocks. We used to dare each other to walk up the river tunnel and emerge inside the factory. We would go part of the way and turn back. I tried the same feat when I was older and found that I got to a point where the tunnel roof was too low to afford passage. The plantin' also had hazelnut trees on the banks sloping down to the river. These provided us with wild treats in autumn.

Surrounded by nature was educational; we knew our trees. There was a large variety around our home. A sycamore tree, with its little bunches of twin fruit that spun around like blades of a helicopter when they fell to the ground, grew in front of our house. Ash trees grew close by and lime trees lined our avenue with a large beech tree on the dam bank. Beside our house grew a couple of horse chestnut trees with the 'horseshoe' on their twigs. Nearby was an oak. The oak tree was sacred to the gods in ancient times and people were loathe to cut one down. The Druids worshipped the oak.

We would collect acorns from it in autumn and 'ink-balls' (gall). If the oak was a holy tree the scots or scotch pine was certainly not. Evil spirits were said to live in its branches which served as broom sticks for witches to fly about the sky. It has a broad bushy crown, bluish needles and small dull cones. Resin and turpentine are made from it and its needles contain vitamin C. A beautiful example of a scotch pine used to stand on your right on a bank near the Marks family's lane as you approached Monkstown village. Unfortunately it was cut down to block the road during the loyalist strike in 1974!

The tall scotch pine is seen in the background here looking towards Monkstown village. It was cut down to block the road during the Loyalist strike of 1974.

The old factory we regarded as our own special adventure play area. On wet days we could play inside the black stone building known as 'the flat roof' where the ground floor was drab and dusty. It was an eerie place at night with its glassless windows and bats flying about.

Some believed it was haunted, that the spectre of a hooded monk had been seen on top of the flat roof at dead of night walking with a candlelight. I never believed this but we did like to scare strangers or visitors by relating this tale and it was a brave one who would venture into its precinct after dark. Only the owl, flying silently overhead on patrol for errant mice, would be at home in the foreboding, derelict, buildings.

Another test of nerve for the adventurous visitor was to walk up the underground tunnel from the fire room in the old factory to come up below the chimney stack in a nearby field. It was a long dark tunnel with water a couple of inches deep in places and some loose bricks underfoot. We kids had done it many times unaccompanied and without the assistance of a light and used to 'show off' to strangers, especially girls. As children we loved to stand beside the tall chimney stack on a sunny day. Gazing upwards as a light cloud would pass in the blue sky, it seemed to make the chimney move, to come alive, and as we walked around it we fancied it was watching us.

There was an occasion when exploring in the grounds of the factory that we discovered a 'new' tunnel. Investigating below a pile of ivy-covered slates and debris the entrance was revealed. Gingerly I led the way straight down about ten feet using hand holds and foot holds then levelling out at a right angle then another seven or eight feet. The tunnel ended half way up a wall looking down into an area we called 'the cellar holes'; a series of underground caverns in the derelict boiler room. The floor of these places was covered in water with broken bricks lying everywhere. But what we found repugnant, the place

At Play

was alive with ugly black frogs hopping about. It was as loathsome as a snake pit and made my flesh creep. We beat a hasty retreat back up the tunnel which must originally have been used as a service port for the boilers.

The old mill was a dangerous place too. I had an experience which nearly cost me my life and I will never forget it as long as I live. At the end of the long room on each floor there was a square metal cased hole, one directly below the other, measuring about $2^1/_2$ to 3ft square. It was probably a small lift shaft for bobbins or cartons. I was about eight years old and was playing with my older brothers and chums when I accidentally stepped back and fell through the hole on the third floor. The human instinct for survival which must have directed my actions can only be described by the word miraculous. Somehow, with lightning reflexes, I managed to grab the floor with my hands as I fell. I screeched for help. My brothers, hidden from view, thought I was joking. My fingers were slipping, slipping, slipping on the white mortar dust which covered the floor and I was screaming, screaming, screaming. Mercifully Roy McFaul, one of our chums, was alarmed and dived to my rescue. He was a good bit older than me and a strong youth. He lifted me clear by the wrists just as my finger tips were at the edge. Another few seconds would have been too late and my slender body would have been dashed to pieces on the debris covered ground three floors below. My mother and father never found out about this incident nor my sisters. It was years later, in my teens, that I would clamber out of a window on this third floor and scale up the wall using narrow toe holds and finger holds to climb onto the flat roof itself. This act of bravado was done again to impress the young ladies! Small wonder that sometimes at night I wake up suddenly in a sweat dreaming of these incidents.

Among the pastimes girls indulged in was something called 'playing wee houses' where little pieces of delph would be arranged to simulate dishes on a table and other substitutes for teapots and kettles would be used, the aim seemed to be playing little mothers. But skipping was the girls' forte. Two girls at either end of the rope would turn it while another girl would time her movement to dive below the moving rope and pick up her steps to skip in time to the rhythm and all the while the turners would recite something about 'Salt, mustard, carry in pepper' (cayenne pepper). When the skipper missed her step she was 'out' and then became a turner. We boys used to join in sometimes but we were never as good at it as the girls were.

My brother Billy and I have always shared a love of railways and steam engines. This goes back to my earliest memory as a child. The Whiteabbey Bleaching Company had a railway siding which ran into a field at the rear of our house at Bleachgreen. I cannot have been much more than two years of age when my older sister Mabel and her chum each gave me a hand and I toddled down the road between them to the level crossing. Out of the siding and across the road came a steam engine. The figure of a small boy waved to us from the foot plate. It was Billy, being given a ride by a friendly driver.

The railway had undergone a major change in this area in the previous decade. A loop line was built at Monkstown (The Greenisland loop). This was an unemployment relief scheme in the early 1930s. It was

At Play

Bleachgreen Siding. — Photograph: Roddie Andrews.

quite a civil engineering feat. John Chambers, who worked on the scheme, told me that in order to achieve the correct elevation the lower part of the loop line had to be raised on giant stilts like a pier. Further up the hill a cutting had to be made at Monkstown. The clay from the cutting supplied the material for the banking lower down. He said Mr A.N. Scott of Jordanstown was the railway's resident engineer on the job. A massive over and under concrete viaduct was built at Bleachgreen to span the Three Mile River. This was opened on 17th January 1934 by the Duke of Abercorn, Governor of Northern Ireland. The reason for building the loop line was to eliminate the practice of having to reverse at Greenisland (formerly called Carrickfergus junction), and thereby give a shorter running time from Belfast to all points north. The scheme provided 350 jobs through the labour exchange.

Now living in Monkstown we can just about see our beloved railway from our bedroom window in the distance between a gap in the factory buildings. At dusk we hear a train far off and looking out catch a momentary red pinpoint of light as the fire-glow reflects on the engine footplate.

It is a mizzly night. Tiny children's feet climb the wooden stairs to bed. We lie and talk in the dim glow of the tiny bedroom oil lamp. Ere slumber claims us the sound of the 12.15am ex-Belfast goods train can be heard beginning the slow climb up the Monkstown bank. The gradient is stiff, 1 in 77, and the line is slippery with rain.

Chuff.. chuff... chuff... chuff then Chu... chu, chu, chu, chuff as the wheels slip. Then slowly it picks up again, chuff... chuff... chuff.. and that is the last thing the children hear as sleep envelops them at last.

CHAPTER 4
The Travelling Picture-Man

When I was a boy I was an avid reader and collector of western stories. These illustrated papers we called 'western comics'; they were in fact boys western stories. A whole business went on in our village swopping these magazines and I was at the heart of it. I never recall buying new copies although these were offered for sale in the post office/newsagents in the village. The cost was prohibitive. Often I have pondered over this fascination with the western genre. Was it because right always seemed to triumph over wrong or was it the instant justice dispensed from the barrel of a gun? Maybe it was the vision of the wide open spaces and the drifting cowboy which caught my imagination.

One of our childhood games was to play at being cowboys. We acted our heroes. Mine was Roy Rogers, my chum's was Gene Autry and his brother's was Tom Mix. The fields around our homes resounded to the cries of bang! bang! bang! as we simulated the gunfire from the Winchester 73 rifles or Samuel Colt 45 revolvers. We also had a curious way of trotting along with our hands held out in front, to imitate riding a horse. Why was it that nobody wanted to play the part of the American Indians?

They did seem to get a bad press but perhaps this was because they always seemed to lose the battles.

At Christmas I always received the 'Buffalo Bill Annual'. It contained true stories of the west and depicted these historical events in full colour plates. I remember reading the story of the battle of the Little Big Horn. This was an occasion when the Indians did win, defeating General George Armstrong Custer. It was due to reading this story that I always remember the date of the battle, 25th June 1876. The book would also contain stories such as the shoot-out at the OK Corral between the Clantons and Wyatt Earp and his brothers aided by Doc Halliday.

My favourite western tale was taken from a schoolbook belonging to my older brother. It was an extract from a story called *The Virginian* by Owen Wister. The tale concerned a tall stranger (The Virginian) who worked as ranch foreman for a Judge Garth. The extract features a journey from a railhead called Medicine Bow over 263 miles of open prairie to the Judge's ranch. The Virginian was to guide a party of visitors from the train depot to the ranch. The description of the wide open plains of Wyoming held me spellbound as a child. 'Medicine Bow did not forever remain in sight. When next we thought of it and looked behind, nothing was there but the road we had come; it lay like a ship's wake across the huge ground swell of the earth. We were swallowed in a vast solitude'. In fancy I saw the tall grasslands, the trail and the blue Wyoming skies.

I searched for this book in many secondhand book stores but to no avail, it was an American book and was published there. Actually the BBC transmitted a series (back in the 60s) based on the book also called *The Virginian,* starring James Drury.

One of the great weekly social events in our village was the Saturday night picture show held in the football pavilion. This was the local football club's hall — a tin structure which also doubled as a community centre. The picture show was put on by the travelling picture-man who, as the name implies, travelled around the country halls with his movie show. His name was Jimmy Magee and he was a stoutish man of average height, pleasant, always a smile, and he always wore a paddy hat (a soft hat) on the back of his head. Usually he advertised the coming attractions on a bill posted midweek on the tin fence surround of the football ground. He always used the euphonious term at the top of his bill:

MJM PRESENTS
(Reminiscent of MGM)

Jimmy who was from Portglenone, also appeared midweek in a van selling ice-cream.

I had never been to the pictures. The cost was beyond the means of our household where there were seven kids. But I received an invitation from my chum's mother to join her and her two sons at the Saturday Night 'Theatre', all expenses paid. This was to be the first of many kind invitations which I always remember.

As Saturday night arrived I could hardly contain my excitement as I tried to anticipate the event. We arrived at the pavilion where a queue had already formed. Feeling was running high. My chum's uncle, who used to do odd jobs around the football club, always stood at the door on 'crowd-control' duty. When the door eventually opened and we were admitted Tommy had to stand guard over the projector and fend off curious hands.

The projector was the first thing I noticed on entering the hall; then the long backless forms used for seating. We took our seats about half way up the building. This was no fleapit (like Joe McKibbins off York Street); it was tidy and clean. A large white screen filled the front of the theatre. Nearly every household in the village was represented by women and kids. There were some men there — not many. The local pub was the usual venue for the husbands.

Soon the lights went out and on came the supporting film — the 'wee picture' as it came to be known. I was enthralled. It was Laurel and Hardy; I can't recall the title. It was during the start when the credits, listing technicians, photographers etc were going up that I received my first piece of education about the movies that I remember to this day. My chum Tommy said, 'The last piece of writing (credit) to go up is "Directed by". After that the picture starts'. I recall we laughed and cheered at the frolics of Laurel and Hardy but there was a hush went round when the main show was about to commence.

The 'big picture' was a western. It was the famous *Stagecoach* made in 1939 about 10 years earlier. The stars were: Claire Trevor, John Carradine, Thomas Mitchell and a young man the movie was to propel to fame, John Wayne. I will never forget the effect that film had on me. First there was the stunning scenery. Shot on location in the Monument Valley, Utah (John Ford's favourite location for westerns). True, it was not the plains of Wyoming but

Claire Trevor and John Wayne in Stagecoach. — Sketched from a poster by Muriel McCullough.

the effect was just as breathtaking. I gazed at the wide distant shot of the narrow, dusty trail through the valley. I was transfixed, eyes riveted to the screen. The giant outcrops, silhouetted against a cloudy sky, where the cloud effect is pronounced due to filming in black and white. The details of the plot almost passed me by. I was following the main theme — the stagecoach and its varied passengers journeying through lonely country with Apache Indians on the war path.

As I look back I can remember the stagecoach and horses racing along the trail chased by the Indians. I recall the Ringo Kid (John Wayne) sitting on top of the coach taking aim with a rifle and I could hardly sit in my seat for excitement when he jumped between the runaway horses and mounted the first and pulled the coach back under control. A cheer went up around the hall. However it was instantly quelled when it was revealed that everyone was out of bullets and the Indians were still coming. Just when all seemed lost a distant trumpet was heard and the US Cavalry arrived in the nick of time. I was on my feet with the rest joining in the thunderous applause. I was only eight after all!

This reminds me about another behaviour trait I discovered in these audiences on subsequent visits. The film had to have a 'good' ending. Woe betide if the 'good ones' did not win or be seen to win in the end. Sweetie bags, orange peel, etc would be hurled at the screen or at those unfortunates sitting at the front. Howls of rage would go up. There would be a rush for the front door; forms would topple over and the projecting equipment was threatened with impending disaster.

On this occasion however there was none of that. Everyone departed peacefully as Magee beamed benignly, a look of contentment on his visage. As I made my way homeward I was starry-eyed. The experience still left me with a sense of wonder. That stunning scenery, those brilliant action shots. It made my idea of the western come alive. The whole moving imagery was still dancing in front of my eyes and would do for a long time.

Today the western has gone out of fashion. Perhaps all that could be said of such a short period in America's history has been said, and it is true that a lot of unbelievable westerns were made. One of the best of the modern films of that period is *The Outlaw Josey Wales*, starring Clint Eastwood and set around the time of the end of the civil war.

Curiously I saw *Stagecoach* not long ago and I still think it was one of Ford's best western movies. And what about the travelling picture-man? I don't know whatever became of him. He seemed to just fade away. Perhaps it was the coming of television in the late fifties. But I still cherish my memories of that innocent time.

CHAPTER 5
The Salvation of Taghera

When I was young there was an old character in our village who rejoiced in the nickname 'Taghera'. Some of the old folk said that originally he had come to the district when a youth as a 'hired out' farm hand and that was all I knew of his early history. When I knew him he lived in a small row of wooden cottages near the crossroads. He had a wife and a number of children, all of them older than me.

To us schoolchildren Taghera was a ubiquitous sight in the village. He never seemed to work anywhere for any length of time, but was always seen about at some labouring job or other. If a drain needed cleaning out he was seen with a spade and shovel. Maybe a hole had to be dug in the road; there he was again with some other old labourer, with a pick and shovel.

He was part of our schoolday lives because on our way home from school we would stop and chat to him and he always had time for a word or two with us. Usually he would pull out an ancient-looking pipe, light it, and sit puffing away talking about his own schooldays. He always greeted us the same way.

'Hello Bully Man.'

'Hello Tam,' we would reply. We never called him by his nickname as we thought it disrespectful to him. Although years later I found out that he liked being called Taghera.

I remember one time he came into a supply of tobacco which lasted for months. Someone had been to the 'Free State' on a bus run and returned with a bag of tobacco. After a few pipes of the stuff it was given to Taghera who didn't mind the off-putting taste.

His outfit was early bohemian. He sometimes wore a suit-jacket reminiscent of the type of suit worn by a demobbed soldier, although I never heard that he had followed a military career. Other times, in its place he would wear an old hacking jacket that one would have associated with horse-riding, although he only ever rode a bicycle! Beneath this he sported an old railway waistcoat with sleeves; he also wore a thick pair of railwaymen's trousers suspended on a sturdy pair of braces. All this was finally held in place with a thick, broad leather belt. On his feet he wore stout heavy boots (never shoes) and the railway pants would be tucked in at the ankles with safety-pins or bicycle clips.

A friend of my own in later years informed me that he had donated the railway waistcoat and trousers as he had been supplied with two pairs of each every year, when he worked as signalman. Taghera also sported an old Hunter watch which he kept in his waistcoat pocket where an old bootlace took the place of a watch-chain.

Now Taghera was known to adopt a very egalitarian approach towards the produce of local farms. One story which testified to this was told to me by the sister of the local Midwife. In those days the district nurse was based in the next village, and at that time most women had their babies at home. Well, Taghera's wife became due in the middle of the night and he had to cycle a few miles for the nurse, who also had to cycle back with him. As they rode across a hill together Taghera asked the nurse if she wouldn't mind travelling the last mile on her own. She said, 'No, of course not.' He then dismounted and, throwing the cycle at the side of the road, disappeared through a hedge with a sack. The nurse said that before she left Taghera's house next morning, he had returned with the sack full of potatoes and insisted that she take some home with her. I understand the neighbours shared also. This act always placed Taghera in my mind, politically, somewhere between Lenin and Santa Claus. Whether he had an arrangement with the farmer or not I never knew.

ooOoo

Now the highlight of Taghera's life seemed to be his drink at the weekend. Saturday night would always see him staggering homeward in the best of spirits — at least the best of spirits appeared to have been consumed. But no, actually he was very fond of Guinness. Before setting off to the pub he was often heard to say that he had a thirst he wouldn't sell for a pound. Some of the more puritanical members of the community looked down on Taghera for his drinking and he, and old Billy his mate, got the name of being the village drunks.

Our village in those days was a quiet backwater. It was not an overtly religious place. There was no village church but there was a Baptist Church Hall which was just across the road from the village pub. People used to joke and say that there were spirits on both sides of the road — Holy Spirit on one side, watered spirits on the other.

There was a tall terrace of houses facing the public elementary school. In one these houses lived two middle-aged sisters who were staunch Plymouth Brethren believers. To us children they seemed very stern ladies — never smiling. Every Sunday, rain, hail or snow they used to walk to the Brethren Sunday School where they were teachers. On the way they delivered a gospel tract — *The Messenger* — to every house they passed (our house included).

Now it was Taghera's misfortune that every night returning from the pub he had to stagger past the door of these two spinsters. They used to lie in wait to ambush him.

'You are going to hell', they would berate him.

Now speech didn't come easily to Taghera in his present state. When he could eventualyl reply he said:

'Goin' to hell? Missus, I'm in hell when I'm listening to you!'

The fact that the Missus was a Miss only added fuel to the evangelical fire. But Taghera was never rude or abusive. He just groped his way past them up the street homewards.

This went on year in and year out. Probably next day Taghera never remembered anything about it. If he did it did not deter him. Next week he followed his natural desire and headed for the pub. But the sisters were not deterred either. They were on a mission, and inexorable as the tide that swamped Canute, there they were again waiting for him.

'You drunken old wretch! You're going to hell!' they cried, as they glared balefully at him. Taghera just waved them aside.

ooOoo

It was on a Sunday morning, I remember, when the news broke that there had been a miracle. My older brother and sister brought the tidings home from the church hall. As the news filtered out the details became clear — Taghera had been 'saved', born again! It transpired that the local Baptist Church had been holding an 'open-air' meeting near the crossroads when Taghera, staggering homewards, had fallen at their feet! That he fell is no surprise — how he came to be converted was certainly miraculous.

My first thoughts were of those two middle-aged spinsters. Here was the business taken virtually from beneath their noses, so to speak, and by the Baptists of all people; and what a catch!

However, I must say at the outset, young and all as I was, I was sceptical. Miracles rarely happened in our village. Now the year our village football team won the McKelvey Cup, when they played in the Alliance League, *that* was a miracle! The whole village turned out, including the pipe band, to welcome the heroes back home. It was a living dream. But Taghera 'saved'? No, I just could not buy that. Visions of a new Taghera walking to church on a Sunday morning, wearing (Heaven forbid) a new clerical grey suit and a Bible beneath his arm. But the rumour persisted throughout the village.

As the days passed I wandered up around the crossroads to see where Taghera lived hoping to catch a glimpse of him. If I could only see him I could judge if the stories were true. But he was nowhere to be seen. The week passed into Saturday and lo and behold! Taghera was on the road again. He was heading out for the night. But where would he go? — both the pub and the church hall (where the Saturday night meeting was held) stood at the end of the village.

The people watched out from behind curtains with bated breath. Taghera strolled nonchalantly on. This was the acid test as they say — would he take left into the pub, or right into the church hall? Alas, it was the pub! Taghera quietly lifted the latch of the tavern door and disappeared inside.

There seemed to be an almost tangible sigh of relief. God was back in His Heaven and human weakness was back on the street. As I look back, the village has gone, Taghera has gone, the spinster sisters have gone, the pub has gone and a way of life has gone. I can't help wondering though, did Taghera really know that the Kingdom of Heaven had come to Earth that Saturday night, near the crossroads, and he had been part of it?

CHAPTER 6
Shops and Services

At the centre of any community are the shops and services. There were two main grocery and provision stores in the village. Two men between them virtually owned the village. Sam Wilson had the Railway View Stores to the north of the area as well as some houses and fields. James Hagan had the grocery store in the centre of the village, owning most of the centrally situated houses and some fields. These were the post-war years of rationing due to food shortages. A family had to choose which shop in which they would 'leave their ration books' (i.e. which shop to register with). My mother, for some inexplicable reason, chose the store furthest away from us, Sam Wilson's, thus making shopping a bigger chore than it need have been.

These were well-stocked stores with counters running down each side of the shop. Zinc buckets, enamel basins, fire shovels, mop heads, brush heads, hearth brushes and other hardware would be stacked on the customer side of the counter. But the first thing you noticed when walking into the store was the aroma of different smells. The bacon and the cheese and the multitude of other products, because these were the days when most things were bought in bulk by the store and then repackaged by their own staff. Flour, tea, sugar, peas, barley, baking soda, raisins, currants, sultanas, cherries, rice, potatoes, treacle, buttermilk and a host of other products (with the exception of the last two) were all hand-packaged into paper bags. When the product was weighed the bag was folded, not in any old way, but in such sequential steps that the strength of the paper structure was maintained. Weighing did not require particular skill, but Sam Wilson had a set of scales that hung from the ceiling for measuring tea (or sweets) that did require some knowledge and skill. They were a bit like the scales one sees above the Crumlin Road Law Court. It was said they would turn on a pickle of tea. A part of the shelves behind the counter would be fitted out with brown-painted drawers each approximately 12 inches square. They looked curiously inviting to us children and we would have liked to rummage through them. Some were labelled — saltpetre, arrowroot, cloves, sulphur, etc.

Bacon was not sold by the butcher but by the grocer. This was because bacon was regarded as a 'provision' — hence the title 'grocer and provisioner'. A side of bacon would be delivered from the curers and the grocer would cut this into sections with a bacon knife to produce the back-bacon cut, the shoulder-bacon cut and the streaky belly-bacon or breakfast-bacon cut. Cheese had to have the cloth covering peeled off first, then the round cheese would be cut into two round halves. This was done by use of a thin wire with wooden handles at either end. The wire was then pulled through the cheese using the wooden handles.

A grocer was a time-served occupation in those days. He/she had to know about buying as well as selling. For example, if a chest of tea was to be bought, the lid of the wooden chest would be prised off and the tea examined. The grocer when running the tea across a hand would look for plenty of light-coloured specks called orange pekoe — this indicated good quality.

There was no chemist in Monkstown until the early 1960s, but the grocery shops did their best. A glass cabinet in the store would contain kidney pills, liver pills, Beecham's pills, aspirin and Aspro tablets, Mrs Cullen's powders, Beecham's powders, cascara sagrada, syrup of figs, liquid paraffin, an assortment of various types of cough bottle, Vick, Mentholatum, Sloan's liniment, eucalyptus oil, Andrew's liver salts, Epsom salts, peroxide, TCP, zinc ointment, Snowfire, Elastoplast, blades, shaving sticks, Brylcreem, baby powder and God knows what else. Marvellous claims would be made on behalf of some of these brews: 'No, them other ones are not as good. It takes the liver salts to work me'. The same with the cough bottles. People would be at death's door, gasping their last when: 'I got him a bottle of Venos. It put him back on his feet. Niver looked back. Venos ivery time, luv.' Some displayed blind faith in a product with a conviction reminiscent of religious fanatics. There was a belief too, that you had to suffer pain from a balsam if a cure was to be effective. A liniment would be applied to a strained muscle. 'Ahhh, it's working,' groans the sufferer, sweat dripping from the forehead, as the leg is virtually roasted off him. A rub or two of this stuff and the lame and the halt would take up their beds and run! Similar miracles are performed on the football field every Saturday with nothing more startling than icy water (Holy Water?).

As well as a range of fruit and vegetables, both stores would stock drapery and men's footwear (boots). There would be all colours of cotton thread, sewing needles, wool, knitting needles, broad and narrow elastic, buttons, men's '1000-mile shirts' with detachable collars and studs, and also bib and brace overalls. The range of footwear would cover boots for workmen and farmers, and clogs for mill-workers. Leather whangs were sold for laces. A range of Wellington boots was also stocked.

These shops were also general merchants. Both contained large stores for an extensive range of animal foodstuffs, coal, cement, lime, grit, paraffin and petrol. As well as the hardware already mentioned, there would be nails, hinges, padlocks, bars, axle grease for stiff farm carts, spades, hayrakes, garden rakes, shovels, scythe shafts and scythe blades. In those days the blacksmith 'hung' the scythe, joining blade and shaft in a position to suit the user, like getting a suit of clothes made. They sold paint, distemper, paintbrushes and whitewash-brushes and gallon tins of tar varnish.

All weights and measures had to be taken, on a predetermined date, to the British Legion Hall in Whiteabbey to be checked and tested by the Government Department of Weights and Measures. When passed, each item would be crown-stamped in lead with the year date. The Inspector of Weights and Measures could call at any time in a shop and check, for example, that a petrol pump was delivering a true gallon. This did happen from time to time.

A lorry driver was employed to drive the firm's vehicle not only to haul and deliver the animal feeds and coal, but to deliver groceries to outlying parts as well as locally. The shop's representative would go out to the various districts a couple of days a week to collect the orders. These orders would be made up at the store and then delivered about two days later by the lorry. The shops relied heavily on this order trade and it was absolutely essential to their business.

My mother very rarely made an appearance at the shop. The children went twice a week for groceries and there was an order sent up to be delivered on Fridays. Like our family, most people ran a weekly account. Each day you shopped all details were entered in your shop pass-book and this was totalled when you paid each week. The thing we kids remembered most was that when Mr Wilson or Miss Gillespie (the bookkeeper) handed us our book back they always placed a few sweets inside it. A kindly act which meant a lot to children in those austere years of rationing and made the journey home less dreary.

James Hagan was highly respected in the village. There were houses in Monkstown where the husband was out of work in the 1930s slump and the box of groceries was delivered every week even though payment would not take place for years. He had an Armstrong Siddeley car but was mostly seen driving an old Model A Ford. He had one of those quaint two-piece telephones which I used on more than one occasion. I still recall his telephone number: Whiteabbey 3279. His father, James Hagan Snr (we knew him as Jerry) was in charge of the store when we were children. One morning going to school, Granny

Annie Brennan (Monkstown Postwoman).
— Courtesy of Abbey Historical Society.

McNeily next door, gave her two grandsons and myself sixpence and told us to call into Hagan's and get ourselves some warm sweets. It was a bitter cold frosty morning. We presented ourselves at the counter and Jerry asked 'Well?' 'Sixpence worth of warm sweets please.' 'What!' he cried, 'warm sweets! Away and kick your heels in the air and warm yourselves.' And that was that.

Elsie Hagan, sister of James, was the Postmistress and her little Post Office stood near the crossroads. She was a stern, unbending lady. She was also the local newsagent and as well as stationery sold wool, thread, needles, some light drapery and children's footwear. I was destined to become a newspaper boy for her years later, delivering copies of the *Belfast Telegraph* evening paper. Whiteabbey was the local district sorting office when we were children, but Annie Brennan the Postwoman used to sort her mail in Elsie's before starting her round. We would see her as we were going to school in her navy-blue uniform and little navy hat with it's red piping, as she set off with her mailbag on her shoulder to walk(!!) around Knockagh Hill on her rounds. This was done in all seasons and weather conditions entirely on foot, and she was not a young woman. She was succeeded upon her retirement by a Postman, Tommy Gibson, who used a bicycle.

In 1931, John Strange came to Monkstown to establish a shoemaker's shop in a little whitewashed house in the centre of the village. On those quiet days, before heavy motorised transport, you could hear the tap-tap of John's hammer as you walked past his shop. He would be seated at the window, his last across his knees, working at a shoe or boot. John was an excellent craftsman with leather, no

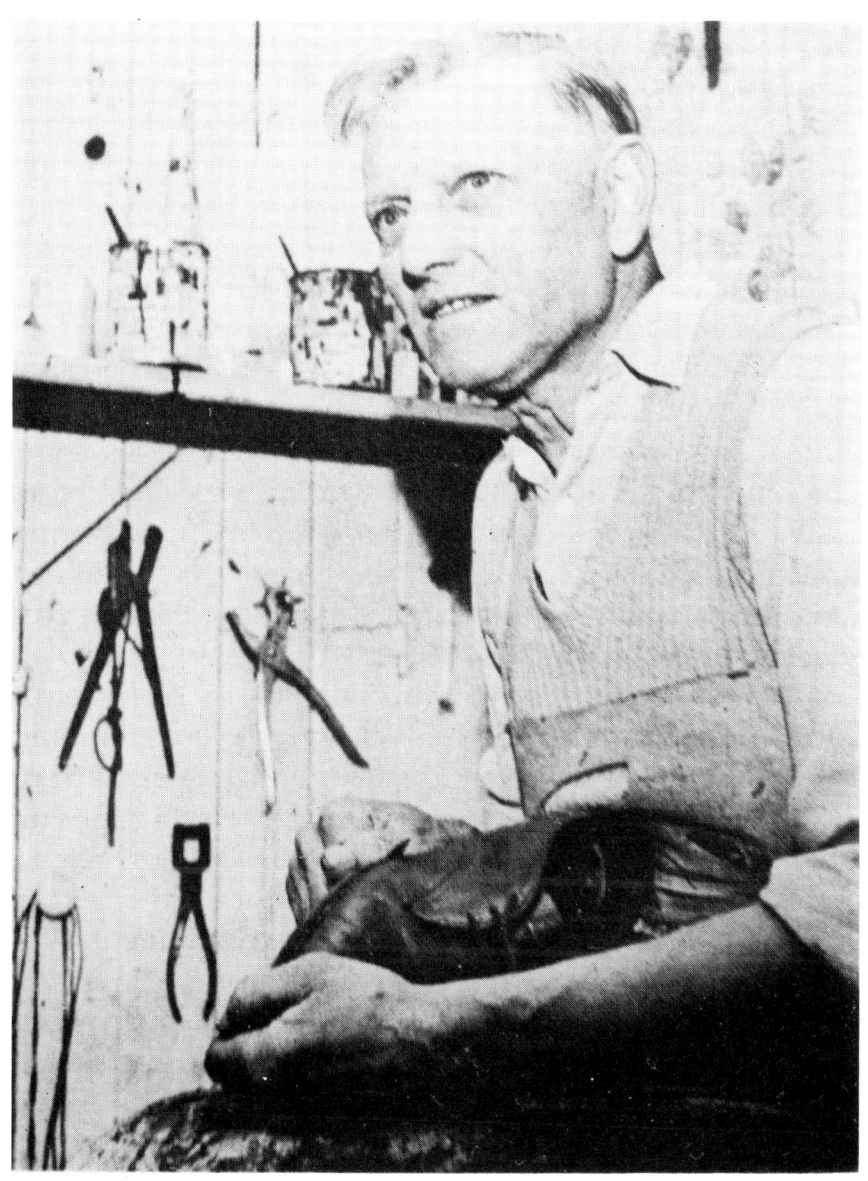

John Strange, the shoemaker of Monkstown. — Courtesy of City Week.

mere cobbler, and he could make shoes or boots when required. When you entered the shop, the smell of leather was evident. He had a machine which consisted of a shaft on which were mounted finishing appliances, the whole being belt-driven from an electric motor. There was a buff for rounding off the edges of new repairs and a wheel covered with a wax-like heel-ball for giving smooth finishes to heels, and a circular brush for polishing.

John was the sort of man people would describe as a gentleman. He was a decent, kindly man and had a fine intellect. As a young man years later, John and I were to become good friends. His tiny shop had a rare quality, for it was a forum where people dropped in to discuss history, poetry, writing, philosophy, art and music. It was an oasis in a desert of barren indifference. Often found seated on the wooden chair by the fireside would be Joe Boyd. Not only did he have an interest in all the topics listed above, but he was a great wit and a character. Joe played the violin and owned an instrument made by Perry of Dublin. He told a tale about Tom Moore who had an interest in fiddles. A young farm-hand from Knockagh called at Tom's house and asked him 'Could ye string a fiddle for me?' 'What make of fiddle have ye?' asked Tom. 'A Stradivarius', was the reply. 'You've a brave fiddle', said Tom without even a smile.

Joe was one of the few people who could charm the spinster Elsie Hagan — he got her to smile. He proposed to her every Tuesday when he called at the Post Office, inviting her to come and live with him in 'a large house overlooking the LMS Railway'. Joe lived in the three-storey houses at School Row! Even when she

Front left: Joe Boyd, Jack Dubois, Joe Peake and Charlie Callaghan.
— Courtesy of Abbey Historical Society.

married, he still kept this up. He got the reputation of being a scribe in the village and people would come to him to get a letter composed, etc. But mischief was never far away with Joe. When the new factories came to Monkstown one very stout lady came to him and asked him to fill in an application form for her. Under the heading marked 'Hobbies', he wrote 'Ice-hockey' (in Monkstown!). Years later Joe and I became good friends. I discovered a softer side to his nature too and I spent many happy hours in his company. He and John Strange became my mentors, guiding me into an appreciation of art, literature, writing and poetry which has always stayed with me.

On 5th July 1948 Aneurin Bevan, Minister of Health in the Labour Government brought into being the National Health Service and Welfare State. This meant free medical treatment, free prescriptions, free dental treatment and free glasses. Care would be provided from the cradle to the grave.

There were no doctors in Monkstown. The bulk of this service was provided by doctors based in nearby Whiteabbey. Two practices mainly served our village, Dr John Doherty's at the upper end of Whiteabbey and the Wilson family practice at Notting Hill, a large house further down the road. There were three Wilson family members in their practice: Dr David, his son Dr Kenneth, and Kenneth's wife, Dr Evelyn. I remember Dr Kenneth Wilson calling at our house on his rounds. He had a friendly, jolly, bantering way with him. 'What are the Andrews brothers up to today?' he would say, set down his bag and immediately get involved with whatever we were playing at, guiders or trains, until he almost forgot why he came. His wife, Dr Evelyn Wilson also radiated gentleness and compassion. They were much loved in the district and people trusted them. They understood and could talk to working people and appreciate the harshness of the daily struggle against poverty and dirt especially in those post-war years. They truly were 'People's Doctors'.

In these times there were no Health Centres, you attended the surgery in the doctor's house. No appointment was necessary, you simply took your place in the waiting-room during surgery hours. When you obtained your prescription you had to take it to a chemist

Shops and Services

in Whiteabbey — there wasn't one in Monkstown. Whiteabbey Hospital was a sanatorium in those days for the treatment of tuberculosis, a deadly lung disease which was rampant in the 1930s. On a Sunday there would be long lines of double-decker buses, queued on the Station Road and along Doagh Road, bringing visitors to the hospital from Belfast and beyond.

These were the days when it was the practice for mothers to give birth to their babies at home, rather than in hospital as it is today. If this happened at night, as it invariably did the husband would have to run and fetch a local midwife, usually a neighbour, and then run or cycle to fetch the district nurse. She was Nurse Gilmore and she lived in a long red tin bungalow at Cloughfern — just about where the Doagh Road entrance to Rathfern is today. Fortunately, she drove a little black Ford car. (I understand she also assisted at my birth.)

On the night of 25th August 1947 we went to bed as usual. I slept in a bed I shared with an older brother. During the night I seem to recall drowsily some commotion in one of the other bedrooms. My brother was sound asleep. No-one came to waken us so I assumed that whatever it was must not concern us and I dropped off to sleep again. Unknown to me there was a crisis. My mother was reaching the climax of a pregnancy. 'Fetch Mrs Peake', my mother said, and my father ran out and brought that faithful old midwife who lived at No 4. She took charge while my father went for Nurse Gilmore and during the early hours of that morning a little son was born. We were surprised and delighted when we came down next morning to find we had a little baby brother. He was to be called Jim after my father.

It was strange that I did not notice the swelling as my mother became due and I could not clearly understand *how* a baby had arrived. I did not believe any of that stork nonsense. It seemed to have something to do with my mother, especially when I saw the baby being breast-fed. A nurse was somehow involved in the mystery too. The thing seemed to be a sort of miracle (but isn't every birth a miracle?). That year Granny Peake was to be busy. Her daughter Mrs Reid, who lived with her, and Mrs Walker who lived at No 6 both gave birth to baby sons. It was a time of prams and nappies.

The neighbours at the Mill Yard. Granny Peake, Mary Andrews, Granny Hewitt with grandson William, Greta Walker, Linda Peake, Muriel Andrews, Billy Andrews, Lizzy Reid and Tommy Welsh.

CHAPTER 7
The Last Refuge of a Scoundrel

An important part of village life in these days when people did not drive and there were no supermarkets was the baker's van calling at the house. There was a variety of bakery firms delivering to our area: Inglis, Ormeau, McWatters, McComb, Mercers, Co-op, Kennedys and probably others. The breadservers were a colourful set of characters with plenty of chat and banter for the housewives and they would have brought the latest news from village to village. During wartime and post-war years, some of them had a drawer in the van where black-market goods were kept for sale. For example, fresh eggs would be obtained from farms at which they called and these would be sold at houses on the round. They tasted much better than the usual dried powdered eggs. Characteristics of the breadmen were the checked, sporty-looking cap and the pencil behind the ear. Most carried a note wallet that both mystified and fascinated us children. They would place a ten-bob note between the two open folds of the leather wallet, simply turn it over, open it again and the note would appear imprisoned behind two broad, crossed elastic bands. Magic! You might overhear a breadserver refer to 'a ticket of loaves'. This was a group of four unsliced, unwrapped loaves, usually loosely joined together.

Tommy Boyd was our breadman and he drove for Mercer. His family was from the village. He was the brother of Joe and, like him, was a great wit and character. Another brother of this family had once climbed to the top of the old mill chimney using the steeplejack's ladders. He sat with his legs dangling over the edge of the stack while he carved his initials on top! Like most of the bakers, Tommy called about twice a week with fresh bread. The customer got a breadbook and the entries were totted up for payment every fortnight or every month.

At about this time there appeared around our village a breadvan with a salesman by the name of Sam Wilkins (the name has been changed to protect the guilty). Where he came from nobody seemed to know, but history has accorded him an entrance akin to that of a biblical prophet, mysterious with a wilderness somewhere in the background. He was above average height, stoutish, black-haired with a small black moustache and red cheeks and he had a certain twinkle in his eye which betrayed an enjoyment of some secret joke. His was a jovial, likeable personality and he displayed a bewitching charm with women and men alike.

Sam came to live in Monkstown. He joined an evangelical church in the district and before long had ingratiated himself into favour there. He settled down with his wife and family. She was a quiet sincere little person who obviously lived in his shadow. It was about this period that his business began to pick up in the village, people switching from merely buying a few pastries to running monthly accounts. Being connected to a church to which others belonged must have helped increase his trade. He would be seen on weekdays on his rounds, a white shopcoat, dark suit and dark tie, like a cleric, with the jolly laugh and that twinkle in his eye.

Meanwhile, back at the church, he had managed to inveigle himself into the position of office-bearer, distributing hymn books and welcoming people at the door with a handshake. Now on this particular morning he spotted a lady leaving after the service, went up to her extending his hand and expressing the wish that she would come back again. Unknown to Sam, the lady was a foundation member of the church! Further, she was Miss Grant, a middle-aged spinster who did not suffer men gladly, in fact she thought, generally speaking, that they were a bad set of fellows. She was a woman in business, she knew the world and knew the importance of caution when extending credit to those of little-known circumstances. Who was this Johnny-come-lately nobody knew anything about, and what right had he to dare to welcome her, a foundation member, and wish that she would come back indeed?

'I have every intention of returning as I have done all my life', she answered him icily, bestowing a look that would have withered lesser men and meant 'Damn your eyes'.

Sam bowed politely, thanked her for her generosity and retired smiling. He had hit an iceberg, but a minor one and he was still afloat. His star was in the ascendancy and he knew it for the twinkle in his eye remained undiminished. He must have been making the right noises to someone because he was presently appointed as a Sunday School teacher.

He got involved in the midweek young people's night. This was a group of young women and men. My brother David, in his late teens, attended at this time and fell under the spell of his enchantment. He thought Sam was a character and laughed heartily at his wit and humour. David was at an impressionable age and Wilkins, in his late twenties or early thirties, was looked up to and admired by my brother. Perhaps it was Sam's tolerant, jovial, man-of-the-world outlook compared with the narrow, dull, sameness of the prevailing type which made him popular with the young folk. That all the time he might have his eye on the main chance never occurred to anyone. Faith can be as blind as love at times. Gaining strength from what he observed as the dumbness all around him, Sam felt emboldened to go a step further. He waited until a wet night arrived then offered to run the girls home. One of the girls, arguably the prettiest, lived two miles further away up a long, dark lane. Sam, a married man, drove her alone and unchaperoned home in the breadvan. I think David felt a bit resentful at this for he fancied the girl himself but had no transport to compete. It was always the boys who left the girls home whatever the weather, but the charisma of Wilkins seemed proof against reproach and he and David became very friendly, and my brother was a guest at his home on many occasions.

The first stirrings which indicated that all was not as it seemed occurred not at the church, but at the home of a respectable family in the village who were not religious. They were customers of Sam's and paid their bills regularly every month to him. Imagine Mrs Scott's surprise when she got an account from the bakery billing her for goods supplied, for several months previous to date. These were the days when homes did not have telephones. She waited and nailed Sam. 'Throw the bill on the back of the fire', he told her assuredly. 'It's a mistake at head office. I'll sort it out.' This placated the worried Mrs Scott for a season, that is until Mrs McKnight, another regular paying customer got a similar bill. 'Don't worry', said the complacent Wilkins, 'they don't know what they're doing at that office. I'll fix it'. The two ladies were neighbours and compared notes. Soon rumours began to circulate that other customers had received similar bills. The finger of suspicion began to point at Sam Wilkins.

The rumours reached our house about the same time as they reached the church. Mrs Scott was related to a neighbour of ours and it was she who warned my mother. 'Tell your son to be careful', she said. 'That man is not all he seems to be.' My mother was astounded.

David refused to believe it. The kindly, faithful old minister was asked by a church committee to approach Wilkins who at this time was holding 'cottage meetings' in his house. These were midweek gatherings for religious zealots who needed a 'top up' between Sundays. Sam protested his innocence to the minister saying it was all a mistake. 'If you are a Christian', he said, 'people are always ready to point the finger. These are unfounded allegations.'

The minister, ever wanting to see the good in someone, reflected on Sam's extraordinary zeal in every facet of church life, his likeable disposition, his earnest plea, his happy home. On the balance it did seem that the rumours were malicious. He apologised for ever having doubted Sam and took his leave.

About a week later Mrs Scott got a 'Before Proceeding To Court' letter from the bakery. She rang the Head Office and all was revealed.

Sam Wilkins had never paid the money in! He was a fraud. Sam's cottage meeting went ahead that night because this news was not yet out. However he must have deemed the game was nearly up and decided to go out in a blaze of glory for he was absent from the meeting but turned up at the end. He entered and the first thing that all noticed was his breath.

The unmistakable smell of alcohol. He had made an attempt to stem scent by eating chips and onion rings but there was no mistaking the devil's buttermilk. Two church members excused themselves in disgust. The unrepentant rascal was more jovial than ever, laughing heartily at his own backsliding. He left in the van to run the same young lady home again!

Meanwhile Miss Grant had been busy. She had heard the rumours and had done a piece of brilliant detective work. She had unearthed a commercial traveller who knew about Wilkins' past. It transpired they had been travellers for the same company. Wilkins had been sacked over money matters and embezzlement. His car and reps bag had been taken off him. 'Was I right or was I right?' she said. 'Men again!'

The Last Refuge of a Scoundrel

It was later in the week when the scandal broke about Sam and the young lady. Whatever he got up to in the van, possibly pressing his unwanted attentions on her, she told her parents and they were furious, threatening violence to his person. Also when the church checked his Sunday school moneybox it had been raided leaving only a 'Free State' penny and an Indian half rupee! It is written, 'Let he who is without sin cast the first stone.' There were many in that church who must have felt like using a technicality in the wording and causing death to Wilkins by a hail of bricks!

To live in a small village with such a scandal was impossible. Like the biblical flight into Egypt, Sam and the family left town one step ahead of the posse. Nothing was heard of their going. It was about a week later a postcard dropped through our letter-box. On one side was a picture of the Liver Birds on the other side the cryptic message:

'ARRIVED SAFELY IN LIVERPOOL.
LOVE TO ALL. SAM.'

There it was, the final two fingers, 'Love to all'. You could almost feel the triumphant twinkle in the eye. Which reminds me why I gave him the pseudonym Wilkins. It was after Wilkins Micawber that wayward character in Dickens' *David Copperfield* that he resembled so much and who was always having impecunious difficulties.

82 Requiem for a Village

Monkstown Public Elementary School Class 1947/48
Back Row (from left): T. Cairns, B. Andrews, D. Marks, T. Luney, N. Whitley, J. Hosick, E. Bell and D. Neil. Next Row (from left): C. Walker, P. Adrain, N. McKee, M.R. Houston, M. Kempton, S. Hunter, M. Curry and J. Brennan. Next Row (from left): M. Forsythe, I. Hewitt, D. Greer, J. McCrea, B. Clarke, E. Houston, I. McMurtry, J. Gourley, B. Campbell and J. McClean. Front Row (from left): B. Cooper, D. Campbell, B. Elliott, M. Russel, M. Gourley and R. Campbell.

CHAPTER 8
The Changing Village

The post-war years of rationing seemed a bit of a puzzle to us children. If Britain had won the war, as was claimed, how come we were still on war-time rations? We were too young to understand of course the full implications of the war in Europe. Land fighting had taken place there causing destruction of crops. With the defeat of Germany came the total collapse of their agriculture industry; Thirty million people were facing starvation. So food had to be directed there and rationing prolonged at home.

Other things that mystified us kids were the ration book coupons. We left these to my mother, all that is except the sweetie coupons. These we fully understood. There were 'D' coupons and 'E' coupons — the former worth two ounces and the latter four ounces. We were lucky because our kindly aunts (my mother's sisters) made great sacrifices and gave us their sweetie coupons and we will be ever grateful for their generosity. Although you had coupons you had to wait until the shops got their confectionery orders in. It was easy to tell when this happened because the wholesale supplier's dark blue van with oval-shaped rear windows and bearing the name 'Nelson' would be seen outside the shops on our way home from school. We knew it by sight. Taking our few saved up pennies we would call at Mary Walker's kitchen shop. Our eyes lit up at the sight of the row of bottled boiled sweets. There were: Black Balls, Aniseed Balls, Brandy Balls, Bulls Eyes and Clove Rock. Mary was sympathetically patient while we made our minds up. We handed over coupons and pence and left with our purchases. Mary was a very gentle lady and sadly was to die a young woman.

An adjective commonly used in these years was 'UTILITY'. It meant standard design which in reality turned out to be basic. Transport used UTILITY buses. These ran on petrol and had seats made from thin wooden slats. In 1947 Christian Dior ended years of women's drab utility clothing with its square shaped shoulders by presenting the 'New Look' fashion in London. This was a more feminine look with the figure-of-eight or hour-glass figure. Some years would pass before it would make its appearance in our village but it did not stop women and men joking and bantering about it. In school we used utility jotters and utility pencils made by The Cumberland Pencil Company, a plain wooden stalk with a graphite centre. Even jotters were not always available as James Stewart (the master) ordered old drawings to be cut up and the reverse side used for doing calculations.

The standard system which prevailed in public elementary schools was a poor system. It failed the pupils in two ways. Because subjects were taught to a standard level at a standard pace there was no provision, on the one hand for those students who excelled the norm, or on the other hand for those who did not, or could not, come up to the standard. No account was taken of individual differences in ability or pace of learning. But the system had even a greater claim to ignominy. Pupils would be caned for not knowing how to solve a mathematical problem or for having poor reading skills! This was totally and unquestionably wrong. Even great girls in their teens were caned by the master, not for misbehaviour but for not knowing! Some of these pupils may have been suffering from dyslexia or been partially dyslectic.

The teachers no doubt were also victims of the system of those times but some managed better than others. If you are meant to teach a broad range of subjects it is hard to excel at every one. But the whole teaching style was wrong too. It was teacher-centred not student-centred. Teaching was done to you; it was dictatorial even with final year students. In an atmosphere where biting sarcasm and caning are used against those who are struggling how could it be possible to engender a love of subject or discover the thrill of learning.

I was fortunate in that I found school work relatively easy and sailed through lessons thus avoiding the sarcasm and caning mentioned above. In fact I managed to skip second standard. But this led me to become a victim at the other extreme. I had to pass four years in the top standard (seventh) before I could leave because the law insisted that one must stay at school until the leaving age at fourteen years. With hindsight it would have been better if I had left earlier and gone to technical college but my parents did not consider this at the time. Getting food on the table was deemed more important and that meant getting a job to earn money. I sat my leaving certificate exam in my final year at Glengormley Secondary Intermediate School. This was the Elementary Certificate being examined in: English, Geography, Drawing and Arithmetic which I passed with Credit. They say that your schooldays are happy days. I was glad to see the end of my days at school and have never regretted leaving. My departure from Monkstown Public Elementary was in June 1955, aged fourteen. About three years later the change-over to secondary schools took place for children eleven years and over.

Monkstown Public Elementary School Class 1957
Front Row (front left): R. Greer, I. Bowman, D. Bowman, W. Cooke and A. Stewart. Second Row (from left): M. Hewitt, R. Hunter, J. Jones, Y. McClenaghan, C. Knox, O. Hewitt, B, Salters and J. Lowry. Third Row (from left): B. Stewart, B. Adrain, K. Marks, H. Sloan, B. Heron, M. Hilcock, M. Andrews, R. Adrain and J. Watt. Fourth Row: J. Stewart (Master) K. Heron, V. Dowey, G. Lusk, J. Hillock, R. Clarke, E. Heron, B. Bill and D. Duff.

The mid to late fifties became a period of much change not only in Monkstown but throughout the country. First, the rationing ended in 1954 bringing the post-war era to a close. The ready availability of petrol was to bring about the demise of horse-drawn transport and gradually those sturdy, great, shiny beasts with their hairy feet began to be a rare sight on the roads. They were to be replaced on farms by the now ubiquitous grey Ferguson tractor. Cars also started to appear but they were still the prerogative of the business and professional type and of course the wealthy. Farmers too started to acquire cars but the working populace still used public transport; cars for them were still some way off. But Jimmy Moore of Knockagh Hill still kept a horse to pull a rarer type of rubber-tyred farm cart when drawing animal feedstuffs from Sam Wilson's store (now R.J. Boyd's). This was the last horse in use up until the mid sixties in our area.

We will pause a moment to look at two sporting events which defied petrol rationing and went ahead. The first was an Ulster Trophy car race held on 10th August 1946 on a road circuit around the Ballyclare area. This was the first international motor race to be held in post-war Britain and competitors at home and abroad participated. The course was lined with spectators from an early hour. I was a child of five but I remember going along with my brothers to 'The Point', a forked junction of the Monkstown and Doagh Roads. Here we were thrilled to watch the endless procession of cars making their way to Ballyclare via the Doagh Road. There were racing sports cars being driven to the event to participate in the handicap race. But the main thrill was seeing the Maserati and ERA racing

88 Requiem for a Village

Prince Bira leads Reg Parnell into the last corner at Ballyrobert during the Ulster Trophy Race on the Ballyclare circuit in 1946. — Sketched from a photograph by Muriel McCullough.

single-seaters being towed on trailers. One memory was of a large policeman — they seemed taller in those days — lifting me up and setting me on top of the finger-post to watch the cars go by. The scratch race was closely fought out between the legendary Prince Bira of Siam and the equally famous Reg Parnell. They came into the last corner at Ballyrobert on the final lap almost together. Parnell tried for the inside line but lost his rear wheel allowing Bira to cross the line 100 yards down the road, three seconds ahead of his rival.

The second sporting event was the Ulster Automobile Club's Annual Knockagh Hill-Climb which took place on the last Saturday in September or the first Saturday in October. It was run over the Knockagh Road on the hill of that name just outside Monkstown. Cars raced up the hill one at a time against the clock. The timed portion of the roads was 1584 yards — just giving time for deceleration before the T-junction. We kids regarded the race as our own for Mrs Gallagher, one of our schoolteachers, was there to cheer on her husband who was a competitor. The whole village turned out for this event. The first two years, 1948 and 1949, saw the mercurial figure of Bobbie Baird, in a variety of cars, set the fastest lap of the day. The two bends to watch for spills were the S-bend about half-way up the hill and the following corner known as the 'Horseshoe Bend'.

Of the famous names who raced here among whom were: C.W. Eyre-Maunsell, C.F.C. Lindsay, J.D. Titterington and Malcolm Templeton, there was only one hero in the eyes of the Andrews children and that was Bobbie Baird. He was proprietor of the *Belfast Telegraph* newspaper and raced throughout Ireland and in England. We listened on our radio at home as he competed in The Leinster Trophy Race in Wicklow on July 1951 driving a Maserati and coming second to a flaxen-haired young driver by the name of Mike Hawthorn. Baird was so impressed by Hawthorn that he chose him as his co-driver for the TT thereby giving Hawthorn his first chance in international racing.

Our most enduring memory of Baird was that day in 1952 at the Knockagh Hill Climb when he spoke to us. It was a wet day and we were down at the bottom of the hill near the starting point. Crowds pressed around the cars as they lined up to wait their turn to go. Then we spotted the gleaming red racing car of our hero. Excitedly we crowded around the car but he did not frown or shoo us away as some of the more snobbish types might have done. Instead he saw three or four bedraggled kids, soaked through but had come to see him race.

'Like to see the engine?' he asked.

'Yes please,' we all said at once.

He pressed a lever inside and smiled as the bonnet shot up to reveal a shining 4.1 litre Ferrari engine.

'Thank you very much,' we all chorused, after our inspection. It was a small thing but it meant a lot to us. He went on to set up the fastest lap of the day. When the news reached us of his death a few years later we were devastated. He had been killed so simply. His car had overturned while practising for a race in England. He climbed out, stood up and refused any medical help. Then he collapsed, a broken rib having punctured a lung, and he died on the way to hospital.

The Changing Village 91

Malcolm Templeton dominated the race for a few years towards the end of the fifties then John Pringle

Bobby Baird in the 4.1 litre Ferrari on his way to setting up the fastest lap of the day at Knockagh Hill Climb 1952. — Courtesy of Belfast Telegraph.

reigned supreme for six years. His 1962 time of 48.77 seconds in a Cooper Climax was never to be beaten and the last hill-climb was held in 1966.

Throughout wartime and the post-war years up to the mid-fifties things did not change much in our village. Family life was still revered. There remained a kind of rural insularity from the outside world and city life. People went about their daily lives much as they always had done. But innovations were coming. The desire to break out of the austerity and drabness of the post-war years, the yearning for colour, the new developments in technology and the growth of teenage culture were to sweep in a wind of change across Britain that would eventually penetrate even our little sheltered community.

But first we had our own private technological revolution in our homes at the mill yard. The coming of electricity. Hurrah for the end of oil lamps, flat irons and primus stoves. Welcome to electric suction cleaners and boilers. As my mother and our neighbours said at the time, 'We didn't know ourselves'. This was in the late fifties.

If there was one single thing which had a fundamental effect on everyone's life in 1958-59 it was the coming of television. True, it had made an appearance earlier at the time of the Queen's Coronation in 1953 but there were only about three houses in the village who could afford it. By the end of the decade nearly every house had one and the large 'H' shaped VHF aerials protruded from every chimney. Television brought culture, education and entertainment as well as news directly into every home. People in places like Monkstown were able to see and hear what was happening in places like London, live at the touch of a button. The stars came into your living room. What the stars wore and the latest fashions were also on display, but everything was still in black and white.

But the first victim of this was community life. It started in a small way at first. People who would maybe drop in on a neighbour for a chat at night would meet in one of the first houses in the street to have a television set.

A Christmas party in the old Baptist Hall in the 1950s.

All would sit and stare at the box in the corner. You did not speak for fear of interrupting a soap serial or spoiling a film or talk over someone singing. Conversation died. The next stage was when everyone had a TV, they each stayed in their own homes to watch. The couch potato was born. You only saw neighbours at the shops or going and coming from work. The closeness was gradually fading. It would take a few years for the process to take effect but things were changing. The following years brought about the demise of the travelling picture show in the football pavilion as the villagers stayed at home on Saturday night to watch television. Another aspect of community life was to end.

This effect was not peculiar to our village, it was nationwide. A report issued on 22nd January 1959 claimed the number of people owning TV sets had increased from 19 million to 24.5 million. Two-thirds of the British population now owned a TV and watched it longer.

Across Britain too Rank reported the closure of large numbers of cinemas.

I was apprenticed to a grocery firm in the village at the time commercial television arrived and I remember well the effect the advertisements had on some shoppers. Generally country people were slow to leave traditional brands and move to unknown or untried products. But the young middle-class housewives who had just moved into some of the new private houses seemed to be brainwashed by TV. Things like Danish Blue Cheese had to be ordered specially and Philadelphia Cream Cheese. After a couple of weeks they would tire of these items and we were left with them on our hands.

'Bring your Daz coupons here', said the poster in the window. There was a publicity onslaught aimed at housewives through TV by the soap manufacturers. It was the beginning of junk mail as coupons, offering a redeemable price reduction in exchange for a purchase of a particular soap powder, were posted to every house. The TV ad would show a woman hanging snow-white shirts on a clothes line. The bloke standing in the background would say reassuringly, 'Yes, Madge knows' and the camera would zoom in on the packet of soap powder. Of course we had to cater for all these whims. There was: Omo, Tide, Daz, Dreft, Surf and others. (The last three are still on sale today.)

'Can you tell the difference between Stork and butter?' asked the voice in the margarine ad. Once again, those who had been happy with Echo now switched to Stork. Commenting on the power of television advertising one man stated that if hobby horse dung was billed on TV people would queue up to buy it.

These years also saw the birth and growth of a new culture for young people who were seeking a new identity and new forms of expression different from those of their parents. As usual the changes began in America. Elvis Presley, already a millionaire at twenty-one in 1956 was in the hit parade with a song called *Heartbreak Hotel*. At the same time, a film called *Rock Around the Clock*, featuring Bill Haley and The Comets, caused quite a stir in Britain, with riots in cinemas and police having to be called to eject youths who were 'Jiving' in the aisles. Rock-'n'-Roll was born. This was four beats to the bar music with a 'back beat' i.e. all four beats were accentuated. There was skiffle music around London featuring such things as washboards in its unconventional line-up of instruments. Lonnie Donnegan was one of its stars, but as the decade wore on Rock-'n'-Roll gradually took over. The term which came into vogue to describe young people was 'teenager'. An industry began to grow around this teenage cult and papers like *Titbits,* aimed at young people, began to appear which featured news of pop and rock stars as well as the hit parade and stories for adolescents.

Usually these changes would have taken years to reach our village. But television had changed all that and we were all caught up in the new culture. I was a teenager myself at this time and I remember, after leaving a girl friend home on Sunday nights, rushing back to catch the hit parade being broadcast on Radio Luxembourg. This was in 1959. The teddy boys made their appearance about this time with their drainpipe trousers, draped jacket with velvet collars, bootlace tie and 'ducks arse' hairstyle. I was never a teddy boy — there were few in Monkstown, but I and many others did wear tight blue jeans, black shirts and lace ties. Another rage at this time was the hula-hoop. This was a circular plastic hoop slightly larger than a bicycle wheel which you gyrated around your waist using hips to sway in time to music. I was useless at it but my brother Billy managed it quite well. An English produced teenage cult film was screened in this year and starred Cliff Richard. This was a film that he probably prefers to forget. It was called *Expresso Bongo* and was a musical satire which included topless girls — daring for those days. I saw the film a couple of years later at the new Alpha cinema in Rathcoole.

Other advances were being made in technology. In 1958 for the first time high fidelity sound equipment was displayed at a radio show. This is what we call stereo today and it never took off in this country until the late sixties or early seventies. Alec Issigonis had invented the BMC minicar in August 1959 and the seven inch EP made its appearance the same year. The development of a small semiconductor device called a transistor replaced the old hot valves in radios and the much smaller transistor radio appeared on the market.

But the young people of this new generation had a conscience too as many marched to Aldermaston under the CND banner to protest against the H-bomb and nuclear weapons. Yes, 'The times they were a-changing'.

The new Alpha cinema in Rathcoole.

CHAPTER 9
Black Sandy's Hat Trick

It was five to twelve and black Sandy Thompson brought his grey Ferguson tractor to a halt on the street outside the Railway View Stores

I glanced at the clock and sighed. We closed for lunch at midday but we were going to be late again. This was Sandy's usual time of appearance, dilly-dallying in at high noon. No amount of hints, cajoling, banter or plain speaking could induce him to shop earlier. The next stage we knew well. He would stand in the hallway of the shop and spend about five to ten minutes perusing the contents of a purse while occasionally skellying through a gap in the frosted glass of the door. Sure enough, even as we gazed, the spectral shape was materialising behind the glass. But Bob (the boss) was going to be firm this time. He strode out to the doorway to lock up for lunch.

'Sandy Thompson, late again!' he exclaimed, as the thin, gaunt figure shuffled into the shop.

'Late again Bob,' agreed Sandy, for nothing could fluster or agitate him. There was something about this nonchalant, contented type of answer that made Bob more exasperated at the man.

'What can we get you Sandy?' he said. 'We're trying to get away for lunch.'

Sandy rummaged through the purse again and produced an old dirty tattered note. I bounced around and had the items, including the sliced bacon, assembled and totted in a trice. He reached over a five pound note and got his change. Was that it? No! Out came another note. Again the exercise was repeated even to the extent of another five pound note. Our change was nearly gone.

'Have you nothing smaller?' demanded the impatient Bob.

'Nothing smaller Bob,' affirmed Sandy, unmoved by Bob's passion.

Just as I was loosening my shop coat in preparation for a sprint to lunch I heard a voice say, 'A bag of pig meal Bob'.

Bob was biting his way through his strait-jacket at this point and making for the bars of his cage. The meal store had to be opened up and the lorry reversed out in order to gain access to the pig meal.

'Give Black Sandy Thompson a bag of pig meal,' yelled the by now angry Bob. Nobody called Sandy 'Black Sandy' to his face. He was referred to as 'Black' certainly. But this was a measure of Bob's frustration. At last we got him away. Twelve fifteen. I shot out of the back yard on my bicycle, turned the corner and almost collided with Sandy making his way to the back door again.

'What is it now Sandy?' I asked.

'Ten Park Drive,' he replied happily, a pound note in his hand.

I pointed to the door and took off before the balloon went up. As I journeyed homeward I reflected on Black Sandy and I tried to figure out what he lived for or got from life. He earned the prefix 'Black' to his name on account of his economy with soap and water. Some said, probably untruthfully, that he had not been washed since the nurse washed him. His head was usually adorned by a cloth cap that had once been grey but was now a greasy black, matching the dusky-brown face and neck. A coat that had once been part of a suit covered a grey-striped collarless shirt and navy serge waistcoat. He wore bib and brace overalls tucked into a pair of ancient, dilapidated Wellington boots — the wellies worn winter and summer alike. Sandy eked out a puny, mean existence on a small homestead on the hill with a few cattle, some pigs and hens.

The thing that fascinated me was Sandy's aimless lack of passion. You could not provoke him to anger or hilarity, maybe a slow smile once in a while, but normally he was sober-featured; not stern, in fact always pleasant. He lived with a bachelor brother and of course his wife. He had married late in life and had no family. I pondered on the courtship of Sandy and his light of love. Would he have held her in a close lingering embrace and sealed their troth with a kiss? Or did they simply make a deal as he would have done in the pig market and slap hands on it? If it was the latter, rumour had it that he got a raw deal and had rued matrimony.

On the occasion when I first encountered his wife, I formed the opinion that the rumour had some substance. Charming is not the word to describe her, in fact 'tartar' springs to mind. She had come to dispute an account for animal foodstuffs which Sandy was supposed to have paid but had not. In language which was choice she wrongly accused the firm of making an error but the boss took no nonsense. He escorted her to the door.

The company I was apprenticed to supplied a lot of farmers with animal feeds, not only the Knockagh Hill, Aldoo, Greenisland and Woodburn, but also to outlying places like Ballylinney, Lisnalinchy, Ballyrobert and Kings Moss. Prices for these goods were very competitive and afforded only a very narrow margin of profit. To begin with the supply business could not be run on a strictly cash basis. It was necessary to run monthly accounts for farmers who in turn paid when their milk cheque came through each month from the Milk Marketing Board. This meant a lot of money lying out for four weeks which was 'dead', though still at risk. By the time handling and delivery costs were met it meant that the overall venture did not really pay. Why then did they bother? They did it to get the grocery orders from the farmers and these did pay well. The firm made a shilling (5 pence) on a hundredweight of meal and made exactly the same amount on a pound of tea without any handling costs or money lying out. This was sometimes not always appreciated by our customers.

Black Sandy played a leading role in a drama every year centred on our store. The plot was as follows. Sandy was allowed credit up to a maximum of half a ton of feeding stuff. It was strict that this was observed. Sandy for his part did his best to try and get away with more. Thus he would quickly build up to his maximum then pay cash for each bag he bought above this. But he would use any and every visit to the store to try and seize a chance for extended credit from any young, green employee. And he got away with it once. The boss went off for a week's holiday every year during the summer and we would take in a couple of young schoolboys in their early teens to help out during this period. Sandy arrived down at the shop during this week near closing time as usual. We were very busy and there was a rush on to get away. He took a stand in the hallway peering through the glass until he discovered all the regular staff were busily engaged with customers.

Then the cunning Sandy played his trump-card. Scurrying around to the meal store he loaded five sacks of feeding stuff on to the tractor, telling one of the juniors to 'mark it in the book, it's for Sandy Thompson'. With that he made good his escape driving away as casually as if nothing was amiss.

The boss was beside himself with rage he returned from holiday to find Black Sandy had exceeded his maximum credit by a quarter of a ton. At first he was going to drive to the hill and fetch back what he could. Then he realised the futility of such a venture and had to give in. Sandy had scored a victory. The next time Sandy came into the shop Bob called him around to the store and gave him a telling off for exceeding his quota. But Sandy, like the cat licking milk, listened but went on licking. I thought I detected a mischievous glimmer in his eyes but the features remained as sober-looking as ever.

'Now that's the last Sandy,' said Bob, referring to the credit.

'The last Bob,' repeated Sandy. 'No more,' emphasised Bob.

'No more Bob,' agreed Sandy. The cat licked on.

Scene two was set in the following year when boss Bob was to take his holidays again. As in the previous year he was leaving his business partner, a woman, in charge. She had taken Sandy's victory as a reflection of her inability to cope in Bob's absence. It would not happen again, she vowed, no sir.

'Be careful,' Bob cautioned before he left, 'Sandy will try it again'.

Intelligence reports coming from the hill indicated Sandy's meal stocks were running low. He would know the boss was on holiday — he always knew. A strike seemed imminent. Meanwhile, the lady marshalled her troops. Always the first to panic when the shop was full she addressed the assembled army thus:

'Boys, there's no need to panic. Be vigilant at all times. If Sandy Thompson appears, alert one of the shop staff who will ensure that there is no feeding stuff without cash payment. No Credit!'

He shall not pass, went the watchword. That week everyone was on alert. If a grey Ferguson tractor drew up to the meal-store a dedicated team of staff descended to check out the customer. Store doors were locked up again as soon as the vehicle was loaded. It got to the point that the junior staff were so enthusiastic that you almost needed a password to get to the bogs. The days came and went and still no Sandy, but we never relaxed our vigilance. The week wore into Friday — where is he? It was like one of those western pictures where the fort is expecting an attack and every soldier knows it is only a matter of time. Like a foxy Indian chief Sandy was out there, biding his time for the right moment, and we could feel it.

The favourite hour would be tomorrow, Saturday, the half day, about closing time. He must come and we were prepared this time.

Saturday arrived, the last day, for the boss would be back on Monday. We were busy all morning in the shop and farmers came for animal feeds. The store was watched carefully right up to closing time and Sandy Thompson did not show up. Had we read the signs wrong? Perhaps we were too hard on Sandy, after all it can't have been easy for him trying to get a living from such a little farmstead. We did not say this, rather our faces said it for us. It was a quarter past one and we were tidying up one or two last entries in the accounts ledger. This was normal practice as farmers would come in from the store and stand behind the counter to reach in the list of feeding stuff they had taken. We were writing up one farmer's docket when we noticed 'turn over' on the bottom. Turning over, horror of horrors, we could not believe our eyes. It read: 'Five bags of pig meal for Sandy Thompson.'

We could not believe it. Sandy had got a farmer who's credit was unlimited, and who was innocently unsuspecting of Sandy's credit barrier, to act as his Trojan Horse. Under our very noses he had pulled it off and scored another victory. Two-nil to Black Sandy. We never thought of another farmer collecting the meal for him. The lady boss was vitriolic in her criticism for she felt she had confirmed the belief that women were the weaker sex through her seeming inability to run things in the absence of Bob. The day ended with 'men' being blamed for 'dithering' even though she had taken the note from the farmer herself!

Another incident occurred some years later featuring Sandy, and concerned his footwear for all seasons, the welly boots. We had moved to new premises at the time further up the Station Road above the railway bridge. The boss had decided to fit metal gates across the outer hallway, to be used after lock-up to discourage wayfarers standing in the porch outside business hours. Unfortunately when it rained it caused rusty water to run off the metal and stain our lovely terrazzo floor. A friend recommended a caustic substance for its removal which I believe was salts of lemon. So one morning early after opening, and before the customers were up and about, Bob painted this acidulous mixture onto the floor of the porch and left it to do its job.

About an hour later Sandy Thompson drove his tractor onto the forecourt and parked. It was an unprecedented early hour for him to be about but, as I reflected later, the man seemed to be psychic. As usual he stood in the porch for about five to ten minutes rummaging through an old purse and checking notes. His entrance into the shop was, to say the least, dramatic. His behaviour was likened to a slow action-replay of someone performing the children's game of hopscotch. I marvelled at what I took to be Sandy's bizarre buffoonery, hopping on one foot, but the boss was not impressed.

'What's the matter Sandy?' he inquired.

'Boots,' replied Sandy, looking down at his Wellington boots. 'Boots?' queried Bob, in puzzled amazement.

'Boots Bob,' said Sandy again, and added, 'burnin' feet Bob'.

He glanced next the porch and back again. Then the boss realised the explanation. Sandy had stood for ten minutes in the porch while the acid had burned through the flimsy soles of his wellies. Now when I say the soles were flimsy actually I mean they were virtually non-existent. They had been worn down to the canvas and the chemical had penetrated the last layer of insoles.

There now followed an operation, almost surgical in its scope and nature, involving the removal of Sandy's wellies. I carried each boot between a finger and thumb, at arms length, to their final interment in the rubbish bin. There was nothing else for it but to supply Sandy with a new pair of wellies.

'I suppose we'll have to give you a new pair,' growled Bob. 'New pair,' agreed Sandy pleasantly, ignoring Bob's tone.

Every pair in the shop was dragged down and tried on Sandy's feet, starting with the cheapest. But the luck of the man knew no bounds. The only pair that fitted was the dearest pair featuring the new cushion insoles. Bob shook his head in disbelief. Black Sandy had scored again to complete a hat trick. But the last one was an own goal.

CHAPTER 10
Rocking it into the Sixties

It was now the sixties. The dependable old Three Mile River still meandered through lush green meadows, flowing below the bridge past our home by the old mill, on its journey to the sea. But other things were changing. A new town had been born on the 1st April 1958 called Newtownabbey, and it encompassed the townlands and villages of the old parish of Carnmoney, including the village of Monkstown. There was no immediate alteration to village life, but other eyes were now focused on the fields and meadows around Monkstown. They saw land ripe for development. In less than a decade the village and its way of life would be gone forever. However, that was still in the unknown future.

Meanwhile the upsurge in sales of consumer goods continued apace. Washing machines were now on the market even though the Whitewell Laundry still advertised as 'The Housewives' Choice'. What helped the sale of new machines was the coming of hire purchase. This was the method by which payments for hire were accepted as instalments for purchase of the article. Usually it was one-third of the total cost down, and the remainder of the payments 'over the hurdles' (by instalments) until

108 *Requiem for a Village*

Monkstown Football Club 1948/49

Back Row: George McMurry, K. Redpath, T. Clarke, Jack Gray, Thomas Porter, Sam Baxter, Jim McCullough, Herbie Weir, William Bell, Bertie Jones, John Dunlop. Front Row: B. Forsythe, W. Rainey, C. Atcheson, J. Houston, J. McLoughlin, J. Graham.

the full price was met. Thus the tick-man became a familiar sight in the village, especially on Friday nights.

There was not much in the way of community activities in the village now. The old football pavilion was falling into disrepair. It had been built by public subscription in the forties and it was our community hall as well. There had been a thriving football team and a Scottish pipe band in those days. Granny Peake, our neighbour, was a faithful supporter at the football matches and her son Joe's wife (Alice) was a great organiser of teas, sales and concerts to raise funds for the football club. The whole community supported these events. I remember as a child seeing a pantomime performance of *Cinderella* put on by a touring troupe of actors. It was a brilliant, unforgettable experience. Now the football team is only a memory and the pipe band has disappeared into oblivion.

Young men and older men would still assemble at the crossroads of an evening for a bit of banter and chat. Young girls would walk around the roads in pairs. There was no youth club, cafe or cinema in Monkstown — only the church hall or the pub — and women and girls were reluctant to go in to the Ivy Inn in those days. There was a dance held in the Orange Hall on Knockagh Road at weekends but we teenagers saw it as an event for older folk. I like many others, was beginning to feel the cramping effect of a small village. On television Rock-'n'-Roll was happening everywhere except in Monkstown, or so it seemed. So we started to cast our eyes further afield to look for night life and entertainment with people of our own age group.

110 *Requiem for a Village*

Star of Monkstown Pipe Band

William Sharpe, Jim Gourley, Wesley Currie, Sam Hosick, Tommy Clarke, Sammy Sloan, Jim Clarke, William Mackie, Stanley Gourley, Frank Armstrong, Joe Hadden, Victor Greer, Same Hadden, Fred Mahon, William Crawford.

Rocking it into the Sixties

Off to Belfast we went to the bright lights. As a child it had seemed a place far away. Now as a group of young men on a Friday night spree we could hardly quell the mounting excitement of expectation as we boarded the bus for the half-hour journey. This was about 1961 and we were all dressed up in our best gear. Ties had to be worn to gain admission to the dance-halls but there was no objection to our winkle-picker shoes which were the fashion at this time. This was the era of the 'dry' dance-halls i.e. no alcohol sold or consumed on the premises. Also no-one was admitted who was under the influence of drink, although there was always one or two who hoodwinked the doorman.

There were many ballrooms in Belfast at this period and we had been to most of them. Among them were the Plaza in Chichester Street with its revolving stage, the Gala in Victoria Street, the Fiesta in Hamilton Street and on a Monday night, the Orpheus above the Co-op in York Street. But the three dance-halls which won our patronage most often were the Boom Boom Room in Arthur Street, the Astor in College Court (off Castle Street) and Romanos in Queen Street. The Boom Boom Room was a new ballroom, very modern and decorative. They had a good resident band called The Barristers (or the Jury) and I remember guest stars such as Billy J. Kramer and Peter and Gordon appearing there. Also I recall Lulu experiencing an embarrassing moment when her skirt fell off during a performance there. The Astor was a good hall too. You came down the stairs onto the dance floor. Many top showbands played there at that time.

My favourite ballroom of them all, and the one I frequented most often, was Romanos in Queen Street. I liked the type of people who went there, an assortment of all classes and creeds. The dance-floor was on the ground level while up above there was a balcony on the first floor giving an excellent view of the dancers below. It was a great spot for eyeing the 'talent' and there was a soft drinks bar too where you could invite your dancing partner to a refreshment and do a bit of 'chatting up' between dances. It was the custom in those days for girls to stand on one side of the floor while the boys stood at the opposite side. Usually we operated in twos, myself and a mate, and having spotted a couple of girls who seemed to be together, we made our play as soon as the music commenced a set of dances.

The dancing ran on Friday night from 9pm until 1am. We always got there early for I was fanatical about bands and music. There would only be a few girls in when we arrived but my eyes were focused on the low bandstand with a fountain on either side. Here the resident band, The Melotones, would be playing all the top twenty songs from the hit parade. They were a brilliant band and were under the direction of Walter Davidson. Belle Crowe fronted the band on vocals but my eyes were riveted on the slim young man with glasses who was playing lead guitar. He would lift the instrument and hold it around the back of his head while still playing a lead part, and never miss a note! This was Jim Armstrong, working at that time as a clerk. Later he would go to America along with Van Morrison in the group Them. Jim is still playing in Belfast today

The Melotones Showband. Top (from left): Billy McCullough, Walter Davidson and Jim Davidson. Centre (from left): Billy McCandless, Belle Crowe and Ernie Talbot. Front: Ernie Shimmings (left) and Ray Cowan.
— Courtesy of Newtownabbey Times.

and he is one of the top rock/blues guitarists in the country. Amazingly Belle is still singing every week in a club in Belfast. There was a connection between The Melotones and Monkstown — the late Ernie Talbot of Jennings Drive played saxophone and clarinet with them, although not during my dancing days at Romanos.

Being early arrivals we were able to make advance connections with any girls who were already there. This always stood us in good stead for later on when the dance was packed. The girls would remember us and lift us for the ladies' choice. Thus we often 'clicked' in this way. As soon as the resident band finished, a top showband would come on and play until 1pm. We would dance all night, never missing a chance to chat up the girls during the slow numbers. When the girl clung tightly to you during a smoochie dance you knew you were leaving her home.

When the dance was over and we had collected our coats we would walk the girls home. There were no cars in those days at least none for working class apprentices like us and taxis were beyond our means. The girls did not expect cars and usually did not mind as long as it was not raining. So we accomplished all on the hoof. But the time passed easily and pleasantly, kissing and cuddling, laughing and bantering until we got them home. If things seemed promising we might arrange a night at the pictures during the week. I recall leaving girls home to Mersey Street in the East End and walking girls home to the Shankill Road. The furthest we ever went was to leave girls home to Taughmonagh away out beyond The Kings Hall. Then we had to walk back to the city centre and finally walk home to Monkstown! On these occasions we would refresh ourselves at the milk machines which were now appearing on the roadsides. By the time we got to Greencastle we had to use the public toilet which used to stand there on the footpath. Passing through Whitehouse we would often meet a policeman on the beat wearing a curious type of night helmet, a bit like those worn by

London bobbies. When I got home it would be about 6am. I would slump into a chair until breakfast time, I was due back at work by 8.30am! Would you believe we were back dancing the following night at The Floral Hall? Where did we find the energy? Cars! Who needed them?

Romanos has long ceased to be a ballroom. It changed its name to Leisure World when it was taken over by a retail firm selling sportswear and leisure equipment. Recently it announced it was to close its doors for the last time and I called in to see again what was left of my old stomping ground. The stage and the fountains had gone of course but the balcony rail on the first floor was still there. I went upstairs and gazed over it to the floor below. In fancy I seemed to hear the music of the showbands again and see the dance-floor packed with ghostly figures, jiving and twisting to the beat.

'Do you come here often?'
'No only in the mating season.'
'Can I have this dance?'
'Are you always so quick of the mark?'
'Am I leaving you home then?'
'Are you out on your gag?' (are you joking?)

The phrases we used then seem so incongruous today. You get the same feeling when you watch a home movie of the seventies and you parade across the screen wearing flared bottomed trousers and platform shoes. Did we really look like that?

But it was still happening back in 1961. The Italians had invaded Britain about this time, not their football team, but their engineering products. These were the colourful, streamlined motor scooters which were immediately adopted by the Mods — teenage groups noted for tidiness, who opposed the leather-jacketed, scruffy motorbike groups known as Rockers. These rival groups would descend on seaside towns in England at a bank holiday to have a punch-up. A near riot would ensue with windows in cafes being broken and police having to escort them out of town. In London each group would have their own cafe with its jukebox and each tribe had their particular favourite pop group to identify with.

My brother Billy was, I think, the first owner of a scooter in Monkstown — a Lambretta. I took advantage of the hire-purchase system and became the second owner in the village to have one — it was a Vespa, powder blue with chrome fittings. Neither Billy nor I were Mods. In fact we dressed more like cowboys with our denim Wrangler jeans and denim jackets, ahead of our time in fashion. We took a delight in pasting transfers of scantily dressed young women on our scooters, maybe a pop or film star. In our colourful display we were a ubiquitous sight in the village and beyond, especially up the Coast Road to the Glens in summer. The advantage the motor scooter had over the motorcycle was that when it rained the scooter's bodywork prevented water from the road and wheels being sprayed over the rider's clothes and feet. Thus you could take a girl out for the night as a passenger and still be smartly dressed.

A favourite venue for taking a female companion to was the new cinema in Rathcoole called The Alpha. It was modern in style with comfortable seating and they brought the latest films. In those days I was dating a nurse from the local hospital and I remember spending the evening

The author on his Vespa scooter. Note the red lace tie.
— *Photograph: Roddie Andrews.*

at The Alpha with her. We were in the back row of the balcony doing what boys and girls normally do. The film was *Gypsy* (or was it *Gypsy Rose?*) and when we came out my Vespa was still where I had parked it beside the cinema. Could you do that today I wonder, and expect the vehicle to be still there, undamaged, when you returned?

In 1962 a fundamental change in the pattern of village life emerged due to the coming of modern factories to the local area. It was a time of economical change both globally and locally. American capital looked to Europe to seek outlets for investment and the Northern Ireland Government at Stormont were offering lucrative packages to entice firms to come to the province. The remnants of the linen industry, which had survived the thirties slump and the Second World War, were now facing their demise in the face of man-made fibres produced by Courtaulds and ICI. Entire factories in Belfast fell to the demolition contractor while a few, like those locally in Whiteabbey and Whitehouse, adapted their premises for a different use. The Monkstown Industrial Estate (actually in the townland of Cloughfern) was built on a large meadow, situated at the junction of the Monkstown and Doagh Roads, which was the property of nearby nursery owner Robert Hugh Kirkpatrick. Another couple of fields to the rear of this meadow were also included.

The first firm to come to the Monkstown Estate was Spaldings, a sports equipment manufacturer. A 100,000 square feet had been allocated on which a factory was built to house production. A small advance factory was built beside it to accommodate Standard Telephones and Cables (Northern Ireland) Ltd, a telephone equipment company, while their main factory was under construction (also on this site). STC's parent company in the USA was the telecommunications giant ITT. A local Monkstown man won the prized contract for wiring and installing the electrics of the main STC factory. He was Gerald Jennings, son of a local farmer after whom Jennings Park is named. His Rotary Electric firm satisfactorily completed the contract and it elevated him to become one of the leading businessmen in the province, heading the successful Rotary Group. The STC main factory was roughly twice as large as Spaldings and it made telephone exchange equipment, step-by-step systems, which were later succeeded by the crossbar exchange systems. They were to employ 3,000 people at their Monkstown plant.

The arrival of the factories had a profound effect on every person in the village, but more so on the women, particularly the younger ones. Firstly, like the old weaving processes, electronics in STC required lots of women with small hands to do the fine soldering required in wiring systems. Secondly, the wages offered were much higher than the old linen mills or shops in Belfast. This meant not only the women who had worked in low-paid jobs applying to the factories at Monkstown, but also women who had never worked out, especially those who had no family or whose children were grown-up enough to leave at home. Thus local women gained, what was in many cases, their first independence; they no longer depended on their husband's wage which was in some cases less than their own. This would lead to the weakening of the bond between husband and wife where the relationship was already shaky. But there were lots of men too in the factories who had come to benefit from the new conditions of employment.

But everything has a price and the American companies never give anything for nothing. A new thing appeared called a 'contract of employment' which each employee had to sign before taking up a post. One clause stated that the employee 'must work overtime as and when required' (STC Employees Contract).

Under the usual employment in Northern Ireland there was no contract. The factories finished on Friday night and did not start again until Monday morning. Any overtime was by choice. Soon it became obvious that overtime was the norm in these new factories and this usually involved weekend working. Some did not mind this, seeing only the extra money, as the firms strove to achieve 24 hours per day, 7 days per week turnover. But the estrangement of man and wife, due to the unsociable alienation of overtime, led to more strains on family life.

Another dehumanising aspect of these methods of production was the use of the American Bedaux's time-and-motion schemes, with work-study 'engineers' using stopwatches to set times for certain jobs. People, more used to the pace of village life, were now thrust headlong into American production methods where the individual had to perform more and more like a machine against the clock. This was at the heart of a bitter dispute in Spaldings factory in the sixties.

The third factory to occupy a site in the Monkstown Industrial Estate was Camco, an American firm making oil drilling equipment. They originally were in a smaller factory at Carnmoney Estate. They are the only firm of the original three on the Monkstown Estate who are still in production there today. A Monkstown man, Bobby Blair, is a production manager with the company, having started as an apprentice with the firm many years ago.

Other changes were taking place in the village at this time. The first private estate of bungalows and houses was under construction at Twinburn on the Monkstown Road and the builder was J. McMillan & Son. A number of executives from the new factories were among the first to reside there. The Ivy Inn was also undergoing a metamorphosis. Ginny Gilmore and family, who had managed the pub for years, left and were succeeded by a family called Martin. The Galbraiths, the people who owned the pub (and also owned another bar in Belfast), sold the premises to a Mr Nelson, a Greenisland businessman, who extended the building and changed the little country pub, with ivy growing around the door, into a more English style bar. This was to attract the patronage of the foremen and staff of the new factories. He also changed the name to The Cat and Fiddle Inn with an appropriate sign depicting this spectacle. James Hagan saw a need in the village and built a block of about six new shops — among them a ladies' hairdressers and Monkstown's first chemist's shop, proprietor Sinclair Dundee.

Since one factory alone employed 3000 people this meant that most of the staff did not live in the village. People came from Whiteabbey, Greenisland, Carrickfergus, Rathcoole and a great many from Belfast. These were still the days when people mainly used public transport to travel to and from work. In the evenings there would be long queues of double-decker buses in the factory estate to take the workers to York Street, Grove, Shankill, East Belfast and other places.

And all these people, men and women, young and old, whose working background was probably the linen mills, shops, heavy engineering or farming, were able to turn out some of the most sophisticated telecommunication equipment of its time. They came as largely unskilled and received only on-the-job training. There would be no GCSEs and very few GCE 'O' Levels, if any, among them. But they picked up and developed their skill producing equipment used by British Telecom and in telephone systems as far afield as Australia. I think that says a lot about the adaptability of Ulster workers in general and Monkstown workers in particular.

CHAPTER 11
Confessions of a Counter-Jumper

While working as a junior apprentice there were certain times when I would be sent out to assist the lorryman with the deliveries. This would be the case, for instance approaching a public holiday, when extra orders had to be sent out before we shut down for the vacation. At other times it was just because he had a heavy load and needed help with the work. I liked these trips out because they gave me a break from the routine of the shop. The lorry driver, Charlie, was a pleasant young man and we got on well. One day I would be the company rep and would call at these homes for the weekly orders. Therefore it also helped me to get to know where the outlying customers lived and to meet them personally. However it was not always the case that I created a good impression.

There was one house in a not-too-distant village where two middle-aged sisters lived which was on our delivery round each week. They were the Misses Carswell and normally they were not at home when we called as they worked in the local mill. We obtained a key from a neighbour who lived in the mill terrace beside them. They

The staff of R.J. Boyd's. Left-right: Jimmy McCrea, Roddie Andrews, Ida Gillespie and Bobby Boyd.
— *Photograph: E. McClune.*

were fanatical about cleanliness and particularly polishing, even the hall of the small kitchen house was gleaming with red cardinal wax. The little kitchen/living room was spotlessly clean without even a crease on a cushion cover. Apparently even in the mill they had their own machine frames shining, bringing in their own Brasso and doing the polishing during the lunch break.

My first visit was during the July fortnight when the mill was on holiday. As we drew up to the door in the lorry I saw a tall, thin, gaunt female standing on a chair cleaning a window. She gave us a withering glare and stepped down off the chair. This was the type who might bend but never break I thought. She disappeared into the house only to reappear with a five gallon oilcan. I was in the process of carrying a stone of potatoes in a coarse sack into the house.

'Stop!' she commanded, 'don't bring that into the house'.

She hailed someone inside and there appeared a small scraggy-looking female, equally as stern, holding an enamel bucket. This evidently was the other sister. The smaller one did not speak but motioned for me to empty the potatoes into the bucket. It was then I realised why I was forbidden entry with the sack — the potato dust would have fallen on the spotless floor. In my nervousness the potatoes overflowed and some rolled away below the lorry. I felt the eyes on me as I scrambled down on my hands and knees and crawled below the vehicle to retrieve them. They looked at each other and seemed to agree that I was a boy worth watching. They left me to fill their oilcan while they went inside to supervise Charlie who was struggling in with a bag of coal. Before they left they cautioned me: 'Be careful boy and don't spill it.'

Now I was standing with our five gallon drum feeding oil into the filler which in turn was stuck in the nozzle of their oilcan, It was a lovely day and I was gazing around me. Suddenly a voice from the doorway cried 'Look what you're doing boy!' It was the tall one.

I glanced down and to my horror the oil was flowing over their can and around my feet.

'Why can't you keep your mind on your work?' said the smaller one. It transpired that my drum of paraffin held slightly more than five gallons while their can held only five gallons exactly. Needless to say the explanation was lost on them. They both disappeared into the house. Charlie, who was going past, winked at me and said, 'Don't worry I'll take the oil in. It's too heavy for you.' Before I could stop him he lifted the can and disappeared into the kitchen with oil dripping all over the floor. A shriek from inside the house confirmed my fears. This was followed by the figure of Charlie emerging at a trot, almost getting jammed in the doorway with the oilcan, a grin on his face. Behind him came the two women with arms filled with newspapers, shooing him out. They laid down a trail of newspapers from the street, through the house, and out to the yard. Charlie then had to negotiate this paper trail again, like the hounds after a hare, with the still dripping oilcan. At last we got away, but not before the two sisters were out with polish and cloths to wax the floor again.

'They're happy at that', said Charlie philosophically. I wondered. If they were happy they looked remarkably miserable, but then again, happiness would not lie easily on them.

ooOoo

The inauspicious start of my acquaintance with the Misses Carswell was not the end of our misfortunes. A greater calamity lay ahead. It was a Thursday, a dull, wet, heavy day. The lorry drove up to the Carswell's and I ran to the neighbours to fetch the house key. Every week they took a bag of coal which was emptied into a coal-hole beneath the stairs. The coal-sacks in those days were made from a thick, heavy jute material and were very expensive. The sacks contained ten stone of coal but when wet, as they were on this day, they were much heavier. Charlie went in first with the coal and I followed behind him with the box of groceries. The only method of entry to the low doorway of the coal-hole was for Charlie to release hold of the sack on his back, spin quickly around and catch the falling bag with his arms to the front of his body and propel it into the doorway. Now it happened on this particular day that as he stepped onto the mat near the doorway, he tobogganed across the polished linoleum floor just at the moment he was releasing the sack from his back. He dived to try and catch the falling coal-sack and nearly received a serious back injury in the process. The sack slid down the papered wall and upended itself onto the kitchen floor.

Now my first concern was for Charlie and any injury he might have sustained. He winced as I helped him to his feet and I insisted that he lay on the sofa to rest for a minute or two. He declined and we turned to survey the damage. A large black stain showed on the wallpaper where the wet coal-sack had slid down. The mountain of coal on the kitchen floor had to be 'shovelled' by hand into the coal-hole leaving a pile of wet coal-dust on the floor. Charlie proceeded into the small scullery and emerged again with a dishcloth which he promptly applied to the black wallpaper. The only result of this was that he made the stain larger and caused some of the paper to peel away. He flung the by now black dishcloth into the sink, seized a brush from the coal-hole and began brushing the coal-dust under mats in the kitchen.

'We must get on,' he said. 'Sure you know they'll clean it later.' I tried to suppress a fit of nervous giggles as I thought of those two dragons coming home from the mill to face the damage to the wall. We will get it in the neck for this, I thought. We had to report the incident to the boss when we got back, laying stress on the mat slipping on the polished floor. The boss was sympathetic and he feared Charlie being off work with an injured back with possibly a claim against himself. He went through about ten cigarettes in five minutes as he listened to our report. 'Don't worry about it', he said as he sucked and blew at the fags, but anxiety was on his visage. He knew the Carswells and the inevitable confrontation that lay ahead.

Sure enough, that very night the two sisters took it in turn to watch the main road through the village which was Bob's route home from work. They flagged his vehicle to a stop and almost dragged him into their house to inspect the damage. What transpired can be more easily imagined than described. It must have been a harrowing experience for even the next day Bob was visually shaken.

'The damage is bad', he reported. 'We'll have to paper the kitchen.'

'Whitewash it', suggested Charlie, with a wink in my direction.

'They would never entertain that idea', said Bob, totally missing the joke. As predicted, he had to pay to have the kitchen redecorated.

I never knew whether I was deemed culpable in the coal incident, but a few months passed before I was sent out on the lorry again. However, this did not stop me getting up to another prank involving those indomitable ladies, the Carswells. A complaint had been received from them about potatoes being too small — 'potmarbles' was the description they had used. The boss told me to pick half a stone of large potatoes for them the following week. Charlie and I conspired to pick a 'special' bag of spuds. We searched through about half a ton of tubers until we found four giant spuds which together weighed half a stone and dumped them in a sack for the Carswells. Bob was ambushed again on the way home.

'What's the meaning of this?' demanded she of the taller stature, and produced our 'special' pack for inspection. Poor old Bob had to return to the shop and bring back some normal-sized potatoes.

'I wouldn't be surprised if that boy had something to do with this', she said with pinpoint intuition.

'You know what the young ones are like nowadays', said the boss with a non-committal air.

'Ah!' she replied in affirmation. Needless to say, next day I received a well-earned reprimand.

ooOoo

Another escapade occurred about this time involving me and my bicycle which had only one brake and that not very effective. I called every day with three sisters, dear old ladies, to see if they required anything from the store. Then at lunchtime on my way home I would deliver any item they required. Now the meal-break sometimes was shorter due to late shoppers so I was always on a rush down the road home. With the skill and practice born of necessity I found I could negotiate the wide gate into the back yard of the large house, at a fair speed, and manage to draw up and stop exactly at the back door to deliver my order. These kindly old ladies had a lodger, a gruff, distant, snooty old boy who worked in the Civil Service and drove a large Rover car.

On this particular day I was later than usual. I bent the bike well over as I swung left through the pillars into the back yard intending to make a wider than usual sweep to the door. To my horror the first thing that met my gaze was the lodger standing at the front door of his car. What followed happened in micro seconds. I braked hard but nothing happened. The lodger, sensing danger, displayed a hitherto unsuspected agility which defied his years, dived into and across the front seat of his car as I catapulted past pinning the car door against his feet with my handlebar. In avoiding the car I was forced to propel through a low laurel hedge, in through the open kitchen door, past a bemused Miss Agnes, and finally shot halfway up the stairs before coming to rest.

I did not need a black box recorder to determine the cause. It was excessive speed and virtually no brakes. When I climbed out of my wreckage the first person on the scene was Miss Annie. She displayed a mixture of emotions. Admiration for my skill in performing the manoeuvres; consternation at how close they had all come to ending their days in wheelchairs and compassion for me and my injured bicycle.

'Bless us o!' she exclaimed. 'Are you hurt Roddie?'

'No, not too bad thank you Miss Annie,' I said, extricating a piece of laurel bush from my torn trouser leg.

'I think you go too fast at times', she said laughing, glad that I was not injured. They were comic ladies and they wore cotton dust caps like the picture on the Bisto gravy packets. I thought of that just then and smiled.

'You wanton young vandal,' cried a gruff voice from the door. 'Do you realize the damage you might have done to my car or to me?' I heaved a sigh of relief at the word 'might' because I feared a major repair bill. As it was Bob was going to have to provide a new front wheel and forks as it was his bicycle I had wrecked.

'I'm sorry, I could not stop,' I said, apologetically.

'Humph!' he grunted, his face still as white as a flour-bag. Evidently he had not recovered from the energy he had to expend in jumping, with such undignified haste, to avoid injury to his person. Miss Annie called me back as I was leaving. 'Here's a pot of our home-made marmalade,' she said smiling, 'and no more flying.' I thanked her kindly. It was not the first time and it would not be the last they bestowed such gifts on me, and I record my gratitude here.

And poor old Bob had another repair bill. Sometimes I wonder how the man ever made a profit on the business. For my part I think I put the fear of God into more people during that summer on my bicycle than the local clergyman had done in over thirty years of preaching.

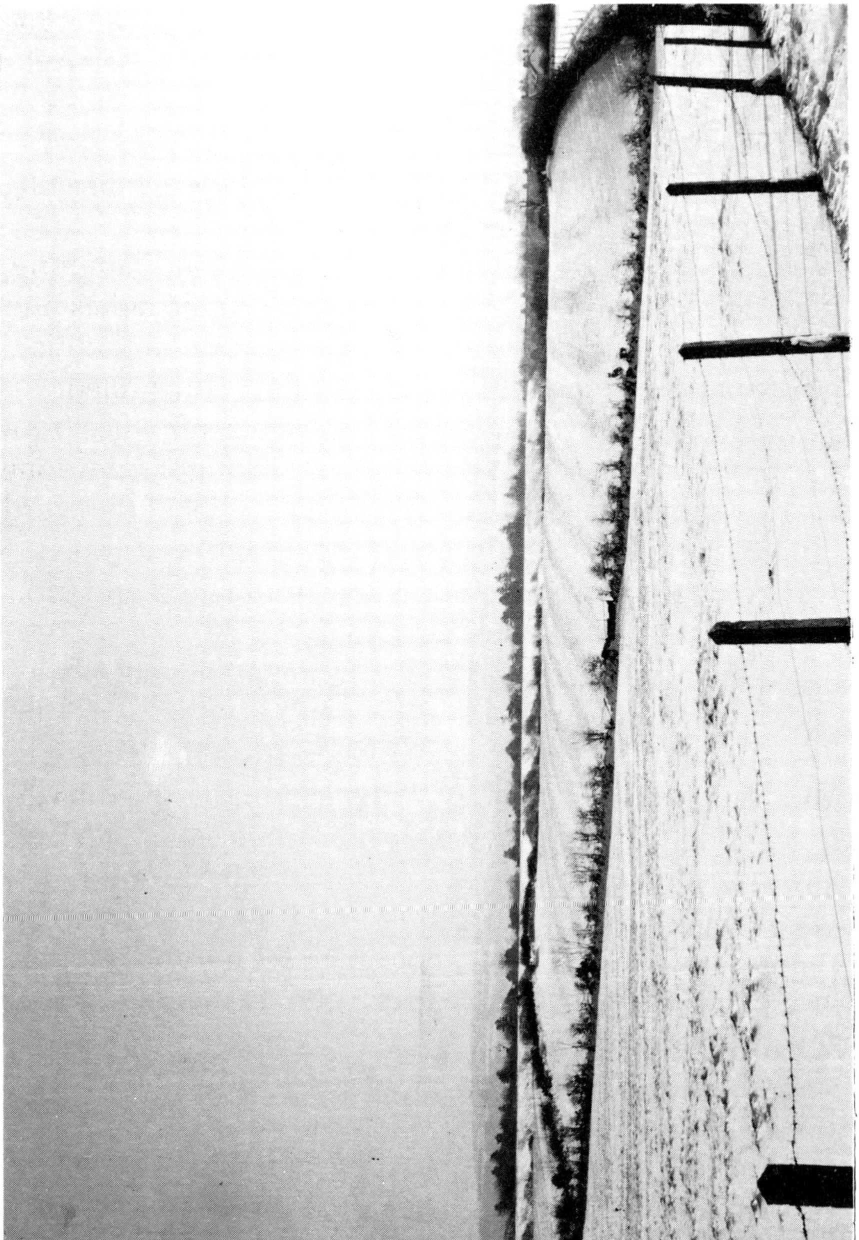

132 Requiem for a Village

CHAPTER 12
The End of the Show

In February 1963 Monkstown found itself isolated for a short time from the rest of the world and the village had to fall back on its own resources. This was when a big freeze-up swept across the North of Ireland, bringing locally the heaviest snowfalls since the previous 1947 cold spell, which had seen the mill dams freeze over. People awoke one morning to find snow had drifted up to the door lintels and all roads, leading to and through the village, were blocked.

My father, like the other commuters, could not get to his work in Belfast, but he and I and the rest of the family turned to and cleared a passage to our garden gate. By lunchtime we had surmounted the high steps leading on to the Monkstown Road and this enabled me to begin the trudge to the general merchant store, where I worked, on the other side of the village. The snow had taken everyone by surprise. Normally at the first hint or threat of snow our firm would deliver a supply of animal feedstuffs to all our outlying customers, in case the lorry could not gain access to the farms during heavy snows. Also, farmers on the local hills would arrive in tractors for emergency cattle and pig feeds if snow seemed imminent. But this time there was little warning. The entire Knockagh Hill and areas beyond were snowed under, with all roads sealed off. However, help was at hand. The army sent a helicopter, which landed at farms, offering to lift hay or feedstuffs to isolated animals or homesteads. They called with a farmer near the Knockagh Monument who assured them she did not need any help as she had enough supplies in store. Farmers are usually prudent and far-seeing.

When I eventually arrived at the store it seemed like the entire village had descended upon us, on foot, for emergency supplies of food, paraffin oil, coal, etc. Husbands, unable to get to work, had been detailed to go to the shops for groceries — not necessarily required, but just in case. Panic buying had set in! Never had we such a constant counter trade and only a small percentage of the customers were regulars. Our own stores were rapidly heading towards depletion and we were about to consider rationing to protect our own clients, when the news came through, about 5pm, that the Monkstown Road had been cleared by a snow-plough. Immediately the boss arranged for our lorry to go to Belfast early next morning to replenish our dwindling stock. Leg weary I trudged home through the deep snow. I had done about a week's work in one day, while the rest of the world seemed to be on holiday.

But other services were working through the emergency. On Thursday 7th February a BEA Engineer at Nutts Corner Airport fell while servicing a Viscount aircraft, breaking a leg and an arm. Once again the army came to the rescue, sending a helicopter to fly the injured man to hospital at Carrickfergus. Unfortunately while returning to RAF Aldergrove the chopper hit the high voltage lines and crashed into a field on Sam McKee's farm near the foot of the Cullyburn Road (now the site of a golf-course). The deep snow-drifts cushioned the helicopter's fall and the pilot was able to climb out of the machine unscathed. His aircraft though, suffered damage and had to be transported back to Aldergrove.

The big freeze lasted about three weeks but once the main roads to Belfast were cleared my father and others returned to work next day. However, the farmers on Knockagh Hill remained snow-bound for two weeks before the tractors and cars got through to the outer world. One of my abiding memories of that time was seeing the caravan of farm vehicles proceeding down the Monkstown Road in single file. The farmers had banded together as a gang and worked from early morning until late on Friday afternoon to clear a tractor path through the road from Slievetrue to Monkstown. They were elated at their success at gaining 'civilization' again and we were inundated once more with demands for much-needed supplies. Some farms farther back beyond the hill, had to suffer isolation for some weeks before they eventually got provisions. One farmer, James Johnstone who lived over near Aldoo, ran out of tobacco and had to smoke tea in his pipe! His animals had not wanted for anything. He said later that he had never been so glad as the moment when he got his hands again on a plug of Warhorse tobacco.

ooOoo

As 1963 wore on Monkstown began to adjust its way of life to the changes brought about by the coming of the new factories. The effect on morals and family life was

A summer excursion train pulls in to lift passengers at Monkstown Halt. — Photograph: Roddie Andrews.

striking. Affairs between men and women became more common and seemed to be mostly centred around the workplace. Such things had been more of a novelty in the village and were more familiar in Belfast. The stress and strains of new working relationships brought about cracks in the marriage structure of some couples. It was inevitable in many ways, when large numbers of men and women were thrown together, for a long number of hours, with weekend working being the norm. But for most families the bond forged in harder times remained firm and unaffected. Television too was responsible for changes in attitude, especially through the influence of the sentimental soap operas such as Coronation Street. But the whole ethos of the village was changing.

Gradually cars began to appear at homes in Monkstown. They were not common yet and new cars were rare. Mostly the vehicles varied from about 2-year-old cars to old bangers about 10 years of age. There was no Ministry of Transport testing of vehicles in these days and provided your brakes, lights, steering and tyres were in good repair that was all the law demanded. This was a time when each brand of car had its unique body design and you could have told a Ford from an Austin or a Hillman from a Morris, easily, without looking at the maker's insignia. After a time it was taken as a sign of status if you had one of these outside your door.

In 1964 I acquired a car and it was certainly no status symbol. It was a 1955 Hillman Minx, red in colour, with the gear lever on the steering column, American style. I had bought it from John Gordon's Garage at Cloughfern for £50, a paltry sum in car terms. This vehicle, with its Irish registration, was to be a familiar sight around the village. I was to become a sort of Toad of Toad Hall, a terror of the highways, around the district and beyond. How the local police must have cursed that Hillman Minx as reports came in of it having been sighted, taking corners 'on two wheels'. The exasperating thing from their point of view was that when they did occasionally catch up with me, on their motorcycles, I was touring along well within the speed limit, all legal and above board. I would be flagged down, asked for documents and the usual examination around the vehicle would be carried out. Then they would tell me that complaints about a car, fitting the description of mine, had been received. This related to 'racing' around the roads — would I make a statement? I blandly denied this and pointed out, with as straight a face as I could manage, that it was just a saloon car! Then I would be cautioned to drive carefully and off I would go to be followed by them for a couple of miles or so. They weren't too bad really, only doing their job.

The local hill-climb 'circuit' on Knockagh Road proved too great a temptation for me. At night I would try and pit my skill against the sharp bends at speed on the Knockagh Road. I would be aided and abetted in this by others who shared my zeal at this form of excitement. The names Brian Percy and Roy Bowman spring to mind here. Mercifully there was still little traffic on the roads on those days, and of course the steep hill slowed my speed considerably by the time I arrived at the 'fast' corners. The only result was an expensive one. Tyres were being burned away at such a rate that every weekend was spent scouring the scrapyards for good second-hand tyres. Strange though it may seem, I never ever had a spill or a crash.

A curious tale concerns the only occasion when my Hillman Minx ended up in the ditch with nobody behind the wheel! My brother Billy and I were taking photographs of some scenic spots near Knockagh and had parked the car in a steep lane beside the main road. We returned around 11.30am to find the car had run backwards into a ditch and was stuck fast. After many attempts to remove it had produced only failure we set off to look for help. The first two farms we called at had nobody home so we walked along the main road in the direction of the next farm. Billy was concerned because he was due to start shift work in Courtaulds factory in Carrickfergus at 2pm and any latecomers were refused permission to start, with the resultant loss of a day's pay. We came to the little Knockagh School at the roadside and I suggested we should seek help in there.

With a certain degree of trepidation I went around to the back door and knocked. Mrs Chambers, the school mistress, answered my knock and listened wonderingly and sympathetically as I explained our plight. She put me at my ease right away. 'Unfortunately,' she explained, 'most of our children are under eleven years of age, but many of them are strong lads who are the sons of farmers. Of course we'll give you some help.' And off we set down the road, the entire school, boys and girls, chattering and laughing in the summer sun. 'You know,' said Mrs Chambers, as we walked along, 'this is just what these kids were probably praying for because we were just about to start some arithmetic problems when you came to the door.'

Eventually we arrived at the stranded vehicle about a quarter of a mile down the road. It looked forlorn and sad and I thought that if my car had a face, like Thomas the Tank Engine, its mouth would be shaped like an inverted crescent moon. I got behind the wheel and Mrs Chambers marshalled her troops to the rear of the car. 'Push children, push,' she called at the precise moment. The car, tyres spinning, slid out of the ditch on to solid ground again. We poured out our gratitude to Mrs Chambers and the schoolchildren and they waved goodbye as we drove off. Billy made it to his work in time to start the shift. When I look back at that event I still smile and wonder that it really happened. It was the sort of thing you only saw in films. But I still remember too the kindness of Mrs Chambers.

ooOoo

The year 1964 brought devastating news to Monkstown. It appeared in the Public Notice sections of the daily and local newspapers and also in the form of a large envelope posted to most households in the area. A Public Announcement was being given that the Housing Trust (forerunner of the Housing Executive) had applied for a Vesting Order for lands within the boundary of the Green Lane, Monkstown Road to its junction with Jordanstown Road, Jordanstown Road up to the railway bridge and the Belfast-Derry main railway line to the Three Mile River. Each home and property owner within the above area was given a map detailing landowners and tenants affected by the changes. The land was to be used to build a large housing estate to rehouse families from Belfast who had to leave the city due to slum clearance. It would also facilitate those working in STC, Spalding, etc. who wanted to move from the city to be near their place of work. Of course people living in Monkstown, whose homes would be demolished due to this building, were to be given first choice of houses in the new estate.

Those of us who loved the village with its rural, scenic setting of green pasture meadows, hayfields, woods and rivers could not take in the news; we were stunned. James Hagan who owned shops, land and most of the village houses affected, appealed against the Vesting Order but his plea was overruled. The death sentence on the old village merely awaited execution. We understood all this of course, but somehow could not bring ourselves to believe it. We continued living from week to week, not looking too far ahead, hoping it might never happen.

At this time we would sit around, groups of us, in cars, listening to the music on the radio. The Beatles were in the hit parade with 'I wanna hold your hand,' but my brother Billy and I were more into the country blues of Hank Williams and we liked a lot of the folk music of that period. We all felt that changes were coming — the village was changing. But we were changing too, growing up, reaching adulthood — things were never going to be the same again. Anyone who has seen the film, *The Last Picture Show* will have an idea of the atmosphere of that time. On Sunday nights we would go down to Pootsie's American Soda Bar at the bottom of the Whitewell Road. Here with the other boys and girls we would play the jukebox and drink Knockout cider (a soft drink). A couple of girls I worked with used to go there and we would meet up sometimes. Billy Poots had created a unique atmosphere and there was never any trouble. Last thing at night, before closing, he would dim the lights and play the No 1 single on the hit parade with the sound turned up to full blast.

ooOoo

Work patterns were changing too. The mufflered men in cloth caps, waiting for the 7am bus to take them from Monkstown to Belfast, grew fewer in number. There were several reasons for this. The last large liner to be built in Harland & Wolffs, the Canberra, was completed in 1962. Approximately 25,000 people were employed there up until her departure. Then came the big redundancy as thousands of skilled workers in the finishing trades were laid off. Only the passenger ships required such large numbers of joiners, plumbers, sparks, etc. The shipyard still had admiralty contracts but the industry worldwide was starting to decline and Harlands was not making a profit on some of its ships. Some of the engineering firms in Belfast, relying on subcontract work from the shipyard, also had to lay workers off.

Another reason for the now half empty bus was that some of the men had found employment in the new factories of Spaldings or STC. And of course there were men who had retired after a lifetime working in Harland & Wolffs Shipyard. Men like Tom Adrain, that great old stalwart of the Monkstown Football Team Committee. But my father still set off in the mornings, stuffing the little oval-shaped tea and sugar tin into one pocket and his small bottle of milk into another, to catch the 7am bus. His friends had tried to coax him to a job in one of the factories. He declined, preferring his work 'down on the island' as he called the shipyard. He was to work there until he retired in 1972.

I followed my father to the shipyard of Harland & Wolff in 1964, the only difference being that I was on the 'staff' — I worked in the offices. The yard was a fascinating place to work in. During my lunch hour I would walk around the huge gantries in The Queen's Yard (known as the Main Yard) where two bulk carriers were under construction. Down these same slipways had slid the mighty *Titanic* and her sister ship *Olympic* over fifty years before. A fact not commonly known was that the grease used to cover the slipway during a launch was a form of soap. It was hired by Harlands from a supply company who charged per barrel. After the launch the soap had to be collected from the slipway, packed into barrels again and returned. I used to pass the invoices for this charge.

Surely one of the greatest challenges to Harland & Wolffs' versatility in engineering must have been the decision to build an oil-rig in the mid sixties, for a company drilling in the North Sea. The design was the product of the shipyard's chief naval architect, Rupert Cameron, who lived in Greenisland. Unlike the Japanese rigs, which had a leg at each corner of a square or rectangular drilling platform, Harland's rig had three legs. The design was innovative in that each leg was a giant tank. The tanks, filled with air, enabled the rig to be towed afloat to her drilling location. Then her tanks would be filled with sea water enabling the rig to rest on the sea-bed. Pumps cleared the tanks again when the rig was required to be towed to another location.

The large drilling platform was built in the Musgrave Yard (better known as the East Yard) and stood high amongst the derricks of the tall cranes there. I attended the launch for I knew it would be a spectacular sight. To slide this giant triangular, three-legged platform into the water would require a lot of mathematical calculation beforehand and fine judgement on the day. The rig was to enter the water apex first, i.e. the single leg first. This front leg was supported on a massive steel box which had been welded together, as a floating pontoon, to maintain the equilibrium of the rig until the two 'aft' legs entered the water.

The vessel was duly named *Sea Quest* and slowly she began lumbering down the ways towards the Musgrave Channel and then something amazing happened. The giant metal pontoon was crushed, like a flimsy aluminium sandwich tin, by the weight bearing on the front leg of the rig! But it still floated and the elephantine vessel entered the channel without a hitch. A cheer went up and the tugs sounded a congratulatory horn at the christening of this huge sea monster.

The *Sea Quest* went on to become one of the most successful oil drilling platforms in the North Sea fields and was one of the first to strike oil there. It was a triumph for Harland & Wolff and in keeping with their tradition of only turning out the best. Those Monkstown men, travelling on that 7am bus to the shipyard, played a part in that triumph and we should be justly proud of them.

ooOoo

The groups of men who had assembled at the village crossroads were gone now. The temporary wonder of television had probably conquered their tired spirits at the end of the day. Somehow community life did not seem to involve the same old commitment any more and a clearer dividing line was emerging between public and private life. The builders had moved in to James Jenkins' fields at Hollybank in 1965 and began the construction of the Monkstown Estate. Not everyone in the village resented its coming, many seeing the chance to leave old houses without bathrooms, etc in exchange for new homes with all modern conveniences. To plead for the preservation of fields, lanes and woods in the teeth of such materialism was futile.

Gradually at first, one or two families left the village and moved away farther into the country. As houses here and there were boarded up Monkstown took on a dilapidated appearance. John Strange closed his little shoemaker's shop in 1966 after 35 years in the village. Towards the end of that year the Housing Trust let the first houses in the new estate.

Soon David Hill would move his butcher's shop down into premises there and Sinclair Dundee would follow with his chemist's shop. James Hagan would not carry on in business.

He would retire and move away to Larne. Sadly the name Hagan — which gave so much to Monkstown — is not even commemorated in a street, road or walkway. Maybe that will be corrected in the future.

One by one our neighbours, with whom we had formed a bond through hard times and through good, left to move to the new estate or other destinations. It was all very sad. Gradually one came to be seen as an anachronism living in an old village house — or so it felt — but our family held on, the last residents in the tall houses in the mill yard. Eventually we had to leave and moved away from Monkstown to a house in the Cloughfern area. Thus it was on 1st August 1967 that my father and I walked out our door at the factory and he turned the key in it for the last time. He said little but I knew his thoughts. The family had been reared there. He had come there as a young married man — now he was 60 and having to uproot.

    The bulldozers moved in with almost indecent haste and two weeks later our old houses were razed to the ground. The rest of the houses in the village soon followed the same fate. Only Riverside Terrace, beside the former public elementary school, has survived to this day.

CHAPTER 13
Monkstown Revisited — and some Reflections

The cold rain slanted down as I made my way up the Monkstown Road. The wind blew in fitful gusts, coming as it usually did in these parts, from the north-west. It was 31 years since our family had left Monkstown and I was on a journey back to observe some of the changes since my childhood days.

Crossing the bridge over the Three Mile River I come to the spot, on the right, where our old terrace of houses had stood, down about 25 feet below the road, in the mill yard. Today the hollow in which the houses stood has been filled in with grass-covered clay up to the level of the road. A well-trodden path across this surface provides a short cut to the Monkstown Estate. As is the way with time-travellers, I pause a while to communicate with a few ghosts.

Beside the road and to the rear of our old home had stood half a dozen lovely old broad-leaved trees — two chestnut, two oak and two lime or linden trees. A wanton piece of authorised vandalism had ordered clay to be filled around the bark of the trees almost half burying them, with the result that they died. My brother Billy protested to the council about this, but the damage was done and it was too late to save them. However, still growing resolutely beside the road are the blackthorn hedges with their pale white May blossom. We used to sample the fruit of these hedges in Autumn, the bitter bluish-black sloes. John McNeill, who lived in Wilsonstown at the other end of the village, used to cut branches of blackthorn to make

The old factory manager's house, home of the Marks family. Jim Andrews is seen in the foreground.

walking sticks. Known locally as the Ballycarry poet, he was a regular sight around the blackthorn hedges which grew in abundance by the old factory. Every time I see the May blossom I am reminded of Patrick Kavanagh's description of a girl having '... dark hair, like clouds o'er fields of May.'

A cold gust of wind disturbs my reverie and I hasten on my way. The two mill dams which lay on the right-hand side of the road were filled in with clay over 30 years ago. The 'big' dam is now a raised piece of green parkway much in use for exercising dogs on. Like a well-trained time-detective I spot the remains of the entrance wall which led to a lane running down to the old factory manager's house. The Marks family, who lived in the house in my time, have four members — Eric, Jim, Molly and Raymond, still living in Monkstown. The old house was demolished years ago.

Farther on, a road leads to the right called Cashel Drive. It lies in place of what had once been a row of black stone houses in the old village, known as Black Row. At the corner of Cashel Drive stands a recently erected building of an amateur boxing club. This is part of the Belfast culture which has permeated this area now since the coming of the large housing estate over 30 years ago. The accent too of the people you meet is a harder type of sound and I notice there is not the same readiness to speak to you as there would have been in the old village. Of course, in a small community you know everyone by name.

Facing the boxing club stands a green painted wooden portable building known locally as 'the green hut'. It stands on what would have been the junction of Black Row and White Row. A notice outside describes it as a 'care centre'. I understand that different care groups meet there, one of which has as its aim to provide a focus for young people's interests and to derive positive outlets for these. This is an encouraging sign.

I bend my steps along Cashel Drive leading into the Monkstown Estate. A girl passing gives up the unequal struggle as the wind blows her umbrella inside out.

'Isn't this weather shocking?' she exclaims, as her dark hair blows across her face. I nod my assent as I render assistance to bring the wayward brolly under control. She smiles her thanks as we part.

The little river with the unimaginative title 'The Pound Burn' flows below the road as I make my way around into Adare Park. These respectable red brick houses and flats stand in what we used to call 'the chimney field'. The large mill stack stood at the corner of the flats and houses which look across to Carnmoney Hill. A little hawthorn hedge used to mark the spot but it has gone. Eric Marks, who lived close by, is reputed to have climbed to the top of chimney by the lightning conductor, hand over hand, like a human fly!

As the warm sun pops out from behind the clouds I am suddenly reminded again of the sheer beauty of the place — the fresh, pale green leaves on the shivering trees and the clear, blue prospect of Carnmoney Hill in the distance; the sound of the burn chattering on its downward course to meet its appointment with the Three Mile River some way off.

Black Row and White Rows (1966). — Photograph: W.M. Andrews.

152 Requiem for a Village

The old mill chimney with the thorn bush growing beside it.
— Photograph: W.M. Andrews.

Monkstown Revisited — and some Reflections

Emerging into Cloyne Crescent (where did they get these names?) the thought strikes me that this area was under crops, corn and wheat, over fifty years ago. As children we would follow the plough, walking along the furrows and picking up the stumps of old cutty clay pipes dropped by ancient ploughmen many generations before.

Digging the sods for Monkstown's first church. Pastor Robert Clarke, David Andrews and Andy Bickerstaff. (All three are now deceased.)

154   *Requiem for a Village*

There were three trees which stood together in the middle of the field like three sisters. They built the present houses around them but only two have survived. One either blew down in a storm or had to be cut down to prevent danger to houses in close proximity to it.

My journey brings me eventually on to Devenish Drive which is the main road through the Monkstown

William Kernoghan pushes the barrow of concrete at the building of Monkstown Baptist Church. The old Ivy Cottage can be seen in the background.

Little Carol Kernoghan steps up to present William McKibben with a Bible at the opening of Monkstown Baptist Church, 1957.

Estate. It follows roughly the geography of the old Hollybank Lane, which led to Hollybank Farm — a cluster of farm cottages which had been situated near the present primary school of that name. On the Jordanstown Road stand two church buildings, near the entrance to Devenish Drive. The Baptist Church, the first church building to be erected in the old village, was built by voluntary labour and opened in 1957. A new church hall was added in 1967. Both building jobs had been carried out under the co-ordination and supervision of William Kernoghan, who is the father of T.&.A. Kernoghan, a firm of local builders. The other church — a newer structure called the Church of the Good Shepherd — is shared by two religious faiths, the Methodists and the Church of Ireland.

The Ivy Inn, once a little country pub, has gone and in its place stand a row of shops. They do bring an improved appearance to the area and supply the local needs. The older Jennings Park houses stand nearby still as good and sound as the day they were built back in the late 1940s.

As I walk up through Ballyalton Park I pass the Moylinney Old People's Home. I know a few ladies from the old village who reside there now. If one has to go into care in old age then it must be a comfort to be among familiar faces and to know that friends and family are not far away. This street takes me up through what had once been the football field where our village team played in the Alliance League — something like the 'B' Division today. Suddenly I am back on Saturday afternoon there and I hear the cheers and shouts of the crowd. My heroes in their black and white striped shirts take shape: Jim Houston (goalkeeper) and his brother John (centre forward), Junior Forsythe, Jackie Gray, Tommy Clarke and Bertie Peake and others. John Houston takes a penalty kick and sinks the ball in the back of the net. A roar of delight goes up led by Granny Peake, a vociferous and loyal old supporter. John Houston, now deceased, went on to play for the legendary Belfast Celtic football team.

My ghosts disappear into thin air again and I take a short cut through some houses to come onto the Jordanstown Road facing the old public elementary school and Riverside Terrace, the only remaining buildings of the old village. Mrs Alice Peake, mother of the previously-mentioned Bertie Peake, lived at No 1 Riverside Terrace. She was a great organizer of social events in the village football pavilion. Her daughters, Gladys and Dorothy, still live in Monkstown. Her son Bertie lives in Mossley.

Riverside Terrace is so named because The Pound Burn flows past the end of the houses. The stream passes beneath the Jordanstown Road here but has for some distance back been enclosed in large concrete pipes, so is no longer visible until it emerges from its subterranean journey near Cashel Drive. My odyssey brings me to the crossroads where I come upon yet another church — Abbey Presbyterian. This is especially hallowed ground for me because the church stands on the site of John Strange's shoemaker's shop — my cathedral of inspiration and learning.

Standing on the roadside looking up at the spire of the Abbey Presbyterian Church it seems to me, from my journey around the area, that Monkstown is not short of religion. However, I suspect religious tolerance might be in short supply. This leads me to reflect on the many conversations I had with John Strange on this very spot. He and I were supporters of the idealism expressed in Dr Alexander Irvine's *My Lady of the Chimney Corner*. We had both been to the small house in Pogues Entry, Antrim, where the story takes place. In a chapter called *The Wolf and the Carpenter*, set in a potato famine in the mid nineteenth century, Jamie (Irvine's father) is caught stealing milk from a cow to feed his starving baby. The farmer, a catholic, does not believe Jamie, a Protestant, and accompanies him to his home to see if his story is true. They find mother and child dying of starvation. Irvine concludes the chapter: 'That night in the dusk, the Fenian farmer brought a sack of potatoes and a quart of fresh milk, and the spark of life was prolonged.' Oh, for more of that tolerance that cuts through the unimportant labels of sect, and extends the hand of friendship to give help where it is needed.

There were two catholic families living in Monkstown when I was a schoolboy. The children of both families attended the village public elementary school along with the rest of us. We laughed and played together and shared our lives. So is religious intolerance only a product of the new Monkstown? But what if one of those catholic families in the old village had wanted to run an Irish dancing class in the football pavilion? I wonder how broad-minded we would have been.

The wall murals, evidenced on my trip around the estate, remind me that the gunmen have not gone away. The slogans testified to a rigidity of outlook, born of that black and white certainty we sometimes ascribe to fundamentalist religions in the Middle East. Yet we are told, following the result of a recent referendum, that we can be more hopeful for the future. But the figures of the hooded gunmen on the gable wall speak more of the politics of despair than hope. Will we live to see the day when this divisive sectarianism will wither away to become nothing more harmless than an embarrassment?

The Andrews family and friends. Back row: Jim Andrews and Pat, a Canadian cousin. Middle row: Billy, David and Mabel Andrews and their friend Elsie McKinty and Roddie Andrews. Front row: Friend Davina Steele, Aunt Jean, Mary Andrews and Muriel Andrews (baby).

That is my hope, especially for the young people of Monkstown.

There is a symbol and reason for hope not far away. It is The Monkstown Community School and it stands at the crossroads almost opposite the Abbey Presbyterian Church. The car park lies on the site of four little wooden cottages and the part of the school buildings which run parallel to Bridge Road stand on the site of what was once Fernview Gardens in the old village. The building is a large red brick structure and was opened in 1976. It is a controlled school of the North Eastern Education and

Library Board and has over 700 girls and boys aged 11-18 years on roll. The school is truly a community school for as well as providing a public library it provides a wide variety of adult classes, a computer club, youth clubs, a senior citizens' club, pre-school playgroup, welfare projects, activities for the disabled, exhibitions, arts and entertainment events.

Crossing the road I enter the building to take a closer look. What a change from the old public elementary school which I attended? The range of facilities I see as I walk around are breathtaking. I am interested to see the facilities we never had at our school such as the two computer suites, the large drama/photography/television studio, the school library, sports hall and gymnasium and the science and technology suites. Some of the pupils have been engaged in a tree-planting, environmental project with Nortel at their telecommunications factory at Doagh Road. The school has achieved very commendable public examination results. Its sporting successes and contributions to sport are well known. Many pupils have gone on to enter universities and colleges of higher education or to highly technical jobs in welfare, trade and industry.

Herein lies the hope. Monkstown is mainly a working class area and the school sources its pupils from primary schools in mainly working class areas. The community school is a doorway for the children of parents who never got the chance to go to university, to take up the opportunity. When they get there they will meet students from other countries around the world. Mixing with these foreign students and sharing experiences, along with their

All aboard! Passengers leaving Monkstown Halt, July 1963 Walter Houston is seen sitting on top of the concrete culvert with a dog. — *Photograph: Roddie Andrews.*

Hollybank Lane. — *Photograph: Roddie Andrews.*

James Jenkins cutting hay at Hollybank, summer 1963. — *Photograph: Roddie Andrews.*

A Twelfth of July party await the train at Monkstown Halt, 1963. — Photograph: Roddie Andrews.

Late evening goods train on the Monkstown Bank. — *Photograph: Roddie Andrews.*

Modern cowboys taking a short cut? The denim-clad Andrews Brothers on their Italian scooters

Hollybank (with its cottages to the right) and Bleachgreen viaduct in the distance. — Photograph: W.M. Andrews.

A GNR steam strain 'trespasses' on NCC lines during summer 1963. Picture taken from Sunshine Meadow. — Photograph: Roddie Andrews.

education, will broaden their minds. If they go to work abroad for a time, as many graduates do, they will get a more worldly view of bigotry and sectarianism and raise their children in a more enlightened way. It can happen because intelligence is not the prerogative of any class.

ooOoo

As I make my way homeward the rain starts again and a white mist shrouds Carnmoney Hill with a penetrating raw coldness. My mind reflects again on the old village. There is always a danger when we reminisce of falling into the traps set by nostalgia. We can so easily drift into the mawkish and sentimental. In the words of Houseman's poem we recall the 'blue, remembered hills'. It is so tempting to describe life in those far-off days as 'idyllic'. But village life also had its down side. Within the kindness there was the suffocating narrow-mindedness of a small community. Our village was not overtly religious, its moral attitude — although not spoken — would be basically Ulster Presbyterian. Sex would not be discussed at home and there was no sex-education at school. It would have been a brave teacher who dared. Adultery would have been frowned upon, the woman regarded as almost a harlot and the man as a leper.

Young people particularly feel the stifling effect of an insular, parochial outlook. I recall an occasion in my late teens, when dressed in tight blue jeans with broad turn-ups, a black shirt and red lace tie, seeing my elders shake their heads in disapproval of my dress style. Hank Williams singing 'My son calls another man Daddy' was described as the 'devil's music'. A friend told me recently that the last witch to be burned in Ireland took place on Carnmoney Hill. The unfortunate victim was dragged from her home in Ballyduff and then taken to the hill to die by conflagration. Clearly there was intolerance around even centuries ago in this area. Some things never seem to change. Yet one man told me, with eyes filled with emotion, that he would give 10 years of his life just to live a for a week back in the village in the old days again. I knew what he meant for I too could feel the unseen tug of it.

What was so brilliant about that time which causes people to yearn for it so? After all they were days of austerity and times of hardship in those years after the Second World War. Rationing did not cease completely until 1954! And we were not 'all in the same boat' as some myths would state, implying there was little difference in incomes. A labouring man with a large family would have the lowest income per capita. A labourer with a small family would be slightly better off. But a skilled tradesman's family could afford luxuries if they were available. These were the days when women were housewives and stayed home to run the household and raise the kids — no small undertaking. Some women did work out in factories. So why the fond memories? I believe it was the sense of *community* which infused our way of life in those days. People felt a responsibility to their neighbours and felt part of the larger village family. Also, they were days of hope. The Labour Government had created the National Health Service — care from the cradle to the grave and everyone had a stake in it.

I remember my mother taking fresh-baked farls of soda bread down to a neighbour. This kindness would be reciprocated another time. When Mary Welsh, our next door neighbour, took her two sons to the cinema I was taken along with them and had my entrance fee paid without any show of condescension. The other longed-for feature of those days was the *caring*. People had time for each other. When anyone was ill everyone rallied around. The neighbours seemed to find time in their busy schedules to have a yarn with each other.

This was especially so where old folk were concerned. The kindness was tangible in so many ways.

It is sad that in today's world people have to work longer and mentally harder and at unsociable hours such as at weekends. All this is driven by a technological revolution which should have made life easier, shorter working week to allow more jobs for everyone. Instead we have the insecurity of short-term and part-time contracts. But where did we lose our way? Was it when the 'keeping up with the Joneses', in the late 1950s became the selfish individualism of the 'I'm all right Jack' in the 1960s? Today husband and wife both have to work out to pay the mortgage, the car and so on. There is little time left at the end of the day for dropping in on neighbours or for looking after old folk. One would not deny the modern conveniences such as the washing machine, television, video or motor car. They are virtually indispensable in society today, and young couples who are starting out usually have to buy a house in order to get a suitable home. But I believe we have paid a high price in social terms and we have lost

The factory houses in the Mill Yard grandly titled 'The Avenue'.

something which was very precious in the *caring* and *sharing* of that community life of long ago.

The rain has ceased as I approach the old townland boundary of Monkstown at the Three Mile River. I stop and turn around to gaze back up the road to where White Row stood in the old village. In fancy, through the mist, I seem to see two figures sitting on chairs at Lizzy Mackie's door. The picture becomes clearer and I see it is old Tom Moore and Joe Boyd. Joe is playing the fiddle and the plaintive sounds of the Irish air *Maggie* come across the midday stillness. Joe used to quote his favourite lines from the ballad:

'The creaking old mill is still Maggie. Since you and I were young.'

I gaze across to where the old Monkstown Factory had stood with its tall mill chimney, and the vision of Joe, Tom and White Row disappear again, swallowed up in the mist. The last few strains of the music are borne away on the breeze.

This is perhaps a fitting place to leave my memories of Monkstown village where I spent such a happy childhood. The journey back in time for me has been a pleasant, therapeutic experience. Maybe reminiscence is a survival technique, a way of coping with this fast-changing world. We can slip back through memory to a time when people mattered more in the pattern of our daily existence. To a period when time itself was not such a precious commodity. While the tear was there, so was laughter too, in abundance.

Bridge Road. The Three Mile River passes beneath the road at the bridge. The little terrace called Bridge Row stands to the right of the road.

APPENDIX
A Walk through Monkstown Village of the 1940s and 50s

Our journey begins on the Monkstown Road after crossing the Three Mile River bridge on the southern boundary. To the right, and standing well down from the road, lie the large houses in the mill yard, and beyond, the derelict factory complete with its tall mill chimney. Access is gained down a stony, tree-lined avenue. Travelling northwards we pass two mill-dams on our right, separated by a lane leading to the mill manager's house. The Marks family live here at this time. I remember during the bitter winter of 1947 these two dams were frozen over and it seemed the entire village had turned out to skate on them!

We come now to the main village with a terrace of black stone houses standing at a right angle to the road — Black Row. Adjoining it and parallel to the road is White Row, a terrace of whitewashed houses. The old spirit grocers building — now two dwellings — stands opposite.

Taking right at the crossroads we pass Elsie Hagan's post office/newsagents, a few houses and then James Hagan's general merchant and grocery store. On the other side of the road are a couple of cottages and adjoining them is John Strange's shoemakers shop (and later to be built beside it, David Hill's butchers shop).

    Proceeding along Jordanstown Road on our left stands Riverside Terrace (nicknamed Teapot Row) and beside it the public elementary school. Facing the school is a split terrace of houses, half of them three storeys high. They are simply known as School Row but the old folk of years gone by had referred to them as The High Street. Next door is the football pitch and the football pavilion. Monkstown has a team that plays in the Alliance League (something like 'B' Division). Facing the football hut are fields owned by farmer Frank Jennings. About fifty houses would be built in these fields towards the end of the forties and they would be called Jennings Park, but known to us kids as the New Houses.

    As we reach the eastern end of the village a lane runs off to the left to Jennings farm and beyond the entrance is an attractive little country pub called The Ivy Inn. This is the only public house in the locality. A Baptist Church Hall stands opposite — there will be no church building in the village until 1957. Just past the hall, on the same side, there is a little slate-roofed house called Ivy Cottage where the Henderson family live. A spout from a stream across the road supplies the water to the premises. Behind the cottage there is an affluent residence which stands on land which had once been a small farmyard where the Duffs — an old Monkstown family — had been reared. Diverting back to the other side of the church hall we see a long lane running down to Hollybank, originally a farm dwelling, now split into small cottages much favoured by young newlyweds as their first home.

Returning to the crossroads we take west down Bridge Road. The neat houses on our right are Fernview Gardens. Further down on our left we pass a group of single storey country cottages known as Spout Row. Below this, on the same side, there is a small farmhouse where people called Addis live. (Jimmy McCrea and family will come to live here.) Just before the river passes beneath the road there stand on the left a little half-doored terrace called Bridge Row and facing this is Mary Walker's kitchen shop. These little shops occupy part of the front room of the house. They are open until late at night and sell sweets, cigarettes and sometimes Paris buns. Minnie Houston also has one in School Row which is very convenient on school days. Dwarfing Mary's shop, with its high banks, is the large pond known as Nellie's Dam. There are a few other houses scattered around the bridge area.

Finally, back to the crossroads again to travel north up Station Road (later to be called Monkstown Road). Parallel to the road , on our left, is a line of wooden huts dating from the First World War. A gap of fields and we come to Sam Wilson's Railway View Stores, a general merchant and grocery business. In later years it will be occupied by Andy's hardware and builder supplies. Opposite this is a large white house, the home of the Misses Hagan — three retired schoolsteachers. Passing by and on the left again a short lane leads down to where Mr and Mrs John Duff have their milk business. The tradition will be carried on by their son Billy. John and the wife are to be seen on a horse and milk float in the village and beyond.

Crossing the railway bridge we come upon a scattering of small houses and cottages. We are on the outskirts now. A lane to the right takes us up to some little whitewashed houses called Wilson's Town, known disparagingly as Hell's Town. Two famous village residents live here. Mrs Brown, the oldest person in the area and John McNeil who likes to be known as The Ballycarry Poet. At the junction with the Carrick Road, and the end of our journey, there are some semi-detached houses on our right. These have been given the unoriginal name of The Villas. This then is the village as I remember it as a child in the 1940s.

Acknowledgement

I would like to record my gratitude to the following for the help they have given me in producing this publication:

The staff of Belfast Central Library and Newspaper Library.

Angelique Day and the Institute of Irish Studies, The Queen's University of Belfast, for permission to quote from the Ordnance Survey Memories of Ireland

Parishes of County Antrim, *Vol 2, (1990).*

Belfast Telegraph for permission to use photographs.

Mirror Group Newspapers Ltd (*Newsletter*) for permission to use photographs.

Morton Newspapers Ltd (*Newtownabbey Times*) for permission to use photographs.

Members of Staff at Whiteabbey Day Hospital, Abbey House who gave me their encouragement and support.

Jim Barker — for the excellent typesetting, friendly advice and help
Charlotte Bradley former librarian at Monkstown library
William Sharpe
Colin Dawson
Bob Armstrong — for his kindly advice and special help
Gillian Shaw
Muriel McCullough — illustrations
Mabel Lindsay — photographs
The Abbey Historical Society — for the use of photographs
My good friend Gerry Rafferty for his indispensable assistance
and any others I have omitted to name.

Many Thanks again.
Roddie Andrews 1998